DONALD SHEBIB'S
GOIN' DOWN THE ROAD

Since its release in July 1970, Donald Shebib's low-budget road movie about displaced Maritimers in Toronto has become one of the most celebrated Canadian movies ever made. In this study of *Goin' Down the Road*, renowned film critic Geoff Pevere provides an engaging account of how a film produced under largely improvised circumstances became the most influential Canadian movie of its day as well as an enduring cultural touchstone.

Featuring extensive interviews with the film's key participants, Pevere provides behind-the-scenes history and explores how the movie's meaning and interpretation have changed over time. He gives special attention to the question of why the film's creative mix of documentary techniques, road movie tropes, and social commentary have proven so popular and influential in Canadian filmmaking for decades.

(Canadian Cinema)

GEOFF PEVERE has been writing, broadcasting, and teaching about film and media for more than thirty years. He is the former movie critic for the *Toronto Star*, co-author of the national best-seller *Mondo Canuck*, and host of CBC Radio's groundbreaking culture program *Prime Time*.

DONALD SHEBIB'S
GOIN' DOWN THE ROAD

GEOFF PEVERE

UNIVERSITY OF TORONTO PRESS
Toronto Buffalo London

© University of Toronto Press 2012
Toronto Buffalo London
www.utppublishing.com
Printed in Canada

ISBN 978-1-4426-4589-9 (cloth)
ISBN 978-1-4426-1410-9 (paper)

∞

Printed on acid-free and 100% post-consumer recycled paper with
vegetable-based inks.

Library and Archives Canada Cataloguing in Publication

Pevere, Geoff
    Donald Shebib's Goin' down the road / Geoff Pevere.

(Canadian cinema ; 8)
Includes bibliographical references.
ISBN 978-1-4426-4589-9 (bound)   ISBN 978-1-4426-1410-9 (pbk.)

1. Goin' down the road (Motion picture)   2. Motion pictures – Canada –
History.   3. Shebib, Donald, 1938– .   I. Title.   II. Series: Canadian cinema
(Toronto, Ont.) ; 8.

PN1997.G64P49 2012   791.43′72   C2012-902250-0

TIFF and the University of Toronto Press acknowledge the financial
assistance to its publishing program of the Canada Council for the Arts and
the Ontario Arts Council.

 Canada Council   Conseil des Arts
for the Arts   du Canada   ONTARIO ARTS COUNCIL
CONSEIL DES ARTS DE L'ONTARIO

This book has been published with the help of a grant from the Canadian
Federation for the Humanities and Social Sciences, through the Aid
to Scholarly Publications Program, using funds provided by the Social
Sciences and Humanities Research Council of Canada.

University of Toronto Press acknowledges the financial support of the
Government of Canada through the Canada Book Fund for its publishing
activities.

Contents

Acknowledgments

There are many people without whom this book would not exist, and I thank them for helping make sure that it did.

For excavating their first-person memories of the production, I thank Jayne Eastwood, Doug McGrath, William Fruet, and, of course, Don Shebib.

For sharing their memories of the film's initial release and impact, I thank Robert Fothergill, Piers Handling, Peter Harcourt, and Martin Knelman.

For identifying potholes along the way, I thank Danielle and Jason Bondy-Sawyer, Randy Cantera, Stephen Cole, Emma Davey, Travis Hoover, Clark Kingsbury, Carol Maloney, Glenn Pevere, and Robert Pevere.

At Union Pictures, I thank Trinni Franke, Cam Haynes, and Robin Cass. Big thanks to the Canadian Cinema series editors Bart Beaty and Will Straw for ignoring all my other suggestions for book-worthy movies and insisting on this one. Good call.

Thanks to Siobhan McMenemy of University of Toronto Press for patience, enthusiasm, and support.

I dedicate this book to Peter Harcourt, the engine-starter.

DONALD SHEBIB'S
GOIN' DOWN THE ROAD

Prologue: A Heavy Rainbow

In a brief shot near the end of *Goin' Down the Road*, Don Shebib's classic 1970 account of dented Canadiana, a man rolls over in a parking lot.

Shebib's first movie is considered one of the most important Canadian films ever made, and his name has been inextricably tied to it for close to half a century. More than once, the filmmaker has expressed indignation at the persistent notoriety of his most famous child. He's proud of it, but sometimes he gets tired of talking about it.

In 2002 Shebib sat down to record a commentary track for the DVD release of his movie. He winced a little in the recording booth when the image flashed by. He'd never been comfortable with the shot.

The man on the ground is a Loblaws grocery clerk. He's just been beaten up by the film's two protagonists – 'knuckleheads,' if you ask Shebib – Pete McGraw (Doug McGrath) and Joey Mayle (Paul Bradley), during a sad attempt to steal food for Christmas. Both men are out-of-work Nova Scotian drifters. One has a baby on the way. They live together with Joey's pregnant wife in a flophouse that smells something awful. Caught while trying to load the lifted groceries into their beat-up old Chevy ('Might as well hang for caviar as hot dogs,' reasons Pete), they club the clerk with a tire iron and take off. A minute or so later, Shebib cuts back to the guy on the pavement.

He didn't want to, but he felt it was necessary for the sake of Pete

Pete (Doug McGrath) and Joey (Paul Bradley). Courtesy of Union Pictures.

and Joey: 'We had to show the audience that he wasn't dead,' Shebib said that day in the booth. 'That would have been far too much of a burden to put on these poor souls.'[1]

Also near the film's end, the not-quite-famous-yet Ottawa folksinger Bruce Cockburn sings about Pete and Joey as 'victims of the rainbow': dreamers who wake up one day to find themselves buried beneath the rubble of their own hopes and desires.

This is Pete and Joey's story. It's the story that Don Shebib wanted to tell, but the parking lot incident ran the risk of dropping one more brick on an already sizeable heap of trouble. If cutting back to the clerk kept murder from the freight carried by the boys, he'd cut back. Pete and Joey might have been losers of a sort – although they, and Pete especially, never give up trying – but they weren't killers. That's a distinction Shebib was determined to make.

The burdens carried by Pete and Joey, the two hard-luck Maritimers who have since become iconic figures in the history of English Canadian cinema – if not English Canadian culture as a whole – are indeed considerable. In the movie itself, the men are shunned, surplussed, sexually thwarted, and turned out on the street. They are chewed up by the cold concrete molars of late-sixties Toronto and shat out the other side, which is where Shebib leaves them: back on the road again, cresting a horizon to a sunset that's already receding. Victims of the rainbow.

Good thing Shebib declined to add a dead grocery clerk to the load, for there would be other burdens to come. On this thin little frame of a movie, made on the streets of Toronto by a four-man crew on a budget of $87,000, much has been heaped. From the moment of its release in the summer of 1970, in a long-gone Yonge Street movie house that had recently wrapped a long run of *Easy Rider* – another shoestring road movie about two guys motoring on the margins – it was hailed as something momentous: the long-dreamed-of beginning of a feature fiction future for English Canada, a paradigm of indigenous cultural expression, an independently fired arrow to the heart of Hollywood – a pure, raw, and soulful expression of what it was to be Canadian.

So it was said.

In the four-plus decades since, *Goin' Down the Road* has been serially canonized as an 'essential' and 'classic' Canadian movie, one without which this country's national cinematic history – a not-uncomplicated proposition itself – would be not only significantly different but differently discussed. Such is the movie's reputation that it has attained the status of near-mythic *ur*-text, with Pete and Joey's plight becoming something of a metaphor for national experience, a foundation upon which almost everything that's been said or thought on the subject of Canadian movies since has been built. It says something that *Goin' Down the Road* is at once so prominent in English-Canadian pop cultural history that it was notoriously parodied by the *SCTV* show in 1982, but not so prominent that the parody probably wasn't more widely seen than the movie. In some respects, it's our belated *Birth of a Nation*, our westward-ho(ser) *Stagecoach*, and our blue-collar *Easy Rider* all packed into one beat up, hundred-buck convertible Impala.

That's some heavy lifting, but lift one must in order to understand how such a small, sincere, and modestly conceived movie, made by a twenty-eight-year-old UCLA film school alumnus of Lebanese-Scottish-Canadian working-class stock, became the cultural touchstone it has.

When one gets back to those roots, after digging through the mountain of positive and negative things said about *Goin' Down the Road* over the decades, after hacking through the layers of iconographic Cancult waxwork that has adhered to it, what you discover is something very small and tiny indeed. A little movie, wonderful in some parts and grasping in others, that is most surprising in its unaffected, hand-hewn modesty, but that arrived in the right country at an exceptionally susceptible moment in its history.

The intersection Pete and Joey pulled up to marked the convergence of much more than the crossing of down-home dreams with Toronto's pitiless reality. It's where a virtual caravan of migrant vehicles pulled up at once, each bearing passengers seeking a place to belong to: a filmmaker who saw no place to make films in his country, a film about a country's domestic refugee class, a cast of actors who didn't act properly, an emergent national culture not certain where it had emerged – but somewhere far from the farms where it was born – a film industry with few films and fewer places to show them. Add to that a virtual truckload of significantly transitory historical moments: the late 1960s/early 1970s; provincial Toronto going metropolitan; out-of-the-closet English Canadian cultural sovereignty; the beginnings of academic film study; a cinematic identity split by customarily sparring categorical polarities: documentary/drama, English/French, Hollywood/Canadian, art/entertainment, publicly funded/privately subsidized, descriptive/prescriptive. It was a pile-up of sorts, and at the bottom of it – or was it the top? – was Donald Everett Shebib's very first feature film.

Not that *Goin' Down the Road* doesn't deserve its lofty perch in Canadian cultural discourse. The point is that the building of that perch says as much about the nature of the discourse itself as it does about Don Shebib's intimate and heartfelt little road movie about knuckleheaded 'poor souls' who can't even get out of a parking lot without fucking it up.[2]

Surfing from Scarborough

At the moment of his emergence as a public figure, Donald Shebib seems suspicious of the attention. Watch him as he sits opposite Pierre Berton (on the late, iconic-in-his-own-right Berton's nightly interview show) in 1972, an incident included on the 2002 DVD release of *Goin' Down the Road*.[1] Hair long and uncombed, dressed in a faded denim work shirt, whiskered and wary, Shebib looks as though he walked off the street and found himself smack in front of a camera. Which in a manner of speaking he did.

Born in Toronto in 1938 to parents of Scottish and Lebanese background, who had come to the city from Cape Breton, Shebib grew up loving sports (especially football), comic books, and Hollywood chestnuts. When television entered his home that TV-mad coronation year of 1952, the young Shebib quickly fixated on vintage movies.

'I got interested in films watching old movies on television,' he told me in 2011. 'And I've never changed. I've only changed a little bit in one way. There was a period I would never watch any film made after 1940. Now I've expanded to maybe after 1950. But after 1950, films went in the toilet.'[2]

At seventy-three, he remembered being particularly devastated by Fritz Lang's 1937 lovers-on-the-lam melodrama *You Only Live Once*. With this power to move him so profoundly, old movies bolstered Shebib's

The Toronto skyline, ca. 1970. Courtesy of City of Toronto Archives, Fonds 124, file 2: f0124_fl0002_id0009.

lifelong fascination with things from the twenties and thirties. 'As much as anything I was interested in the period of the 1920s, the 1930s, which seems the most wonderful time in the world,' he told me. 'Except you didn't want to be old enough to have gone through the horrors of World War I to have to do it. The problem with living in that period was that you got fucked either way. You either got fucked by World War I if you were old enough or if you were young enough you got fucked by World War II.'[3]

The films of John Ford made an impression Shebib would talk about the rest of his life. Frank Capra's movies proved just as indelible. Indeed, if Shebib developed a kind of retro-maverickism, disavowing much of his contemporaries' artistic inclinations as pretentious and silly, it was a stance that was forged in the fertile, black-and-white firmament of the studio system, the products of which supplied Shebib with an abiding sense of what movies at their best should be. When discussing *Goin' Down the Road*, the movie he most often cites as inspiration is *The Grapes of Wrath*.

'If I was in Hollywood during the thirties,' he muses, 'my closest friend would have been John Ford. John Ford and I would have seen things eye to eye. As I would have seen things eye to eye with most of those filmmakers. They were much more salt of the earth people then. I share this, I think. It enables me to not be pretentious and to go for, I hope, honest emotion.'[4]

Back in 1972, as he toughs his way through the interview with Berton, Shebib is a young man out of sync with his moment. He may look like a hippie, but he pines for simpler, more conservative times. He may seem the embodiment of the long-haired contemporary filmmaker – who makes 'socially relevant' dramas and studied at UCLA with Francis Coppola and Jim 'The Lizard King' Morrison – but he really believes movies have mostly been in the crapper since Dorothy opened her bedroom door to a Technicolor Munchkinland. He doesn't like contemporary movies, loves history but hates to read, and speaks glowingly of Murnau's *Sunrise* and classic Capra. Berton is visibly jolted when Shebib admits the movie he'd most like to make is one about turn-of-the-century baseball.[5]

Growing up, Shebib avidly collected things from the past: stamps, comics, sports statistics, model fighter planes. Later on, he'd start acquiring vintage golf paraphernalia. In a sense, what TV contributed to this sensibility was a mechanism for the probing of the obsessively explorable worlds of sport and cinema.

Back on air in 1972, Berton seems determined to tuck the filmmaker into a generation that learned everything it knows from TV. But Shebib – hippie optics notwithstanding – proves an eccentric representative of his generation. While seeming to prove Berton right by admitting he never reads books because they bore him and that he learned everything he knows about literature from *Classics Illustrated* comics, Shebib really couldn't care less about the contemporary. He dismisses most movies of the day as 'pretentious' – a grave Shebibian sin – only allowing to have recently enjoyed, of all things, Franco Zeffirelli's gauzy teenage version of *Romeo and Juliet*.[6]

Not much has changed. In 2011 he said: 'I don't think I'll watch any film made in the 1960s, with that fucking elongated screen. I can't think of a good film offhand other than *Bonnie and Clyde* that was made in the sixties that I liked. Then the seventies got a little bit better and today I don't go to movies at all.'[7]

In 1972 he tells Pierre Berton he used to go through the *TV Guide* in search of movies made in 1939 or earlier, and reveals the dream of a period baseball movie. Forty years later, he sits in his home and tells me that all he watches on his big flat-screen TV are sports and old movies. Capra and Ford remain his most revered filmmakers, and the closest thing to a contemporary nod goes to Penn's forty-four-year-old *Bonnie and Clyde*, a countercultural update of Fritz Lang's *You Only Live Once*.[8]

By the end of the Berton show, a most odd generational reversal has occurred, with the bow-tied establishment broadcasting fixture actually seeming more hip to the times than Don Shebib.

Although an early episode from Shebib's career as English Canada's designated auteur, the Berton interview contains flashes of character that will become tropes of Shebib's public life: the disdain for intellectualism and 'pretentiousness,' the old-fashioned faith in (John) Ford-tough storytelling, the reluctance to accept being the designated representative of Canadian anything (especially Canadian movies, which he'll spend a lifetime ragging), the seething disdain of critics, the testily ambivalent relationship to his own work. These are the characteristics that define what might be called the essential Don Shebib, and they are as intransigently fixed in place as Pete and Joey's greaser-throwback pompadours. Shebib is an old-fashioned traditionalist adrift in a modernist cultural moment, and therefore as much an outsider as anybody he'd make movies about.

After graduating from high school, Shebib enrolled at the University of Toronto to study sociology and history, where he found all that reading drudgery. Although in love with history and the tracing of patterns in the fabric of human affairs, his disinclination towards bookishness put insurmountable limits on his academic horizons.

'When I graduated from U. of T.,' he told me, 'basically my majors were political science, economics, sociology, and geography. Especially human geography. So I was very solidly grounded in the social sciences, and I'm still very much at heart a sociologist. I go nuts when people accuse me or anybody of using generalizations. To accuse someone of that only makes sense when you're talking about a single person in a generalized way. When you're talking about a society you're making generalizations about a general society, and as a sociologist that's what you study.'[9]

'Did you know Patricia Murphy?' he asked me. 'She taught cinema at Seneca College and she once said about me ... "Don thinks and sees things in patterns." I look for patterns. Again that's the sociologist. And so when I started making films my films had a very strong sociological basis."[10]

By the time he graduates in the mid-1960s, he needs to find something to do: something that appeals to his sense of history and sociology but requires minimal academic spadework, something that speaks to his love of the past while allowing him to create in the present, and something that appeals to both his jock and artist impulses. He thinks of making movies.

When one of those exceedingly rare birds called a Toronto filmmaker (Julian Roffman) told Shebib of a movie-making school in California, he packed up and went to UCLA. It was 1961, and there weren't many film schools anywhere, let alone in Toronto. That was the same year he heard director-producer Stanley Kramer speak at the University of Toronto, another inciting event. Kramer's 1958 racial drama *The Defiant Ones* had impressed Shebib as a just about perfect movie, and if Hollywood could still turn something like that out, Shebib had another reason to go west. In California he watched dozens of movies, got his first exposure to foreign cinema, learned to surf, and shared classes with Francis Ford Coppola and, a lifelong friend since, the future director and cinematographer Carroll Ballard (who would contribute to the making of *Goin' Down the Road*). Much as he dug his time at UCLA, where he also did some hanging out with future Doors lead singer Jim Morrison, Shebib felt acutely outside of things. The foreign movies so loved (and invariably imitated) by his classmates were never as impressive to Shebib as the old Hollywood classics, he was the sole apparent Canadian in the fledgling film school, and if the times were a-changin' he wasn't convinced it was for the good. But he remained close with Ballard, and the two collaborated frequently as classmates.

Shebib's first movie was about surfing. Ballard shot it, and it bore, in embryonic form, the style and sensibility that drive and distinguish the filmmaker's coming documentary work: a fascination with subcultural communities on the margins, a respectful appreciation of people who live by codes unappreciated by mainstream society, and a keen eye for the brute engagement of subject and environment. At film school, and in documentary, Shebib found a medium for the articulation of his most deeply animating concerns: the study of people stubbornly striving on the outside, of outlying communities bound by codes and rituals that exclude them from the larger world but provide them with meaning and purpose in the smaller one. He was something of a romantic anthropologist at heart and, were it not for the timing and location of his birth, might have become a devoted director of westerns, a genre built around the spectacle of stubborn resistance against larger forces.

'Which is also the basis of making *Goin' Down the Road*,' he says. 'I saw the sociological pattern between the migrant workers going from Oklahoma to California. It was just a standard city mouse/country mouse thing that happens. Poor people from Sicily going to Rome. The standard story. So I'm very aware of sociological patterns, and much more so than the average person. I see things and see trends that nobody else has ever seen. I was always a really brilliant history student and that would have been my career if I hadn't have done this. But I didn't like to read. That was my big flaw. I was at the top of every history class I was in and I always blew the professors away because they always used to say, "I had no idea you had such a historical grasp."'

'Because I would see the pattern,' he added. 'You only need a certain amount of things to say, "You know, this is what makes sense," and once you have an overview of history and understand how societies function, you can read between the lines and tell the whole story.'[11]

After convincing the National Film Board to assist in the finishing of his UCLA thesis film – a portrait of Toronto street evangelicals called *Revival* – Shebib returned to Canada to begin a highly distinguished early career as a vérité-influenced documentarist, often tackling subjects that involved groups of men in regimented, tightly bonded communities. It began with *Surfin'* and *Revival*, and persisted through *Satan's Choice*, *Basketball*, and *San Francisco Summer 1967*.

Apart from their blunt fascination as contemporary cultural documents, what's compelling about Shebib's pre-*Road* documentaries is their attitude of empathetic but detached engagement. It's the communities and their codes that rivet the filmmaker's attention, not the activity around which the community itself adheres. He may have loved surfing, for example, but the sport itself is oddly incidental. It's what it provides outsiders by way of fellowship and ritual that counts.

In this sense, *Revival* is even more striking. While Shebib could hardly be confused with an easy convert to Christian fundamentalism, he's nevertheless unambiguously impressed by the folk on the corner and their monumentally optimistic mission: to deliver the word of their God to the mostly indifferent and sometimes outright hostile passersby in Toronto, and to continue doing so because the faith in what they're doing is so much stronger than the grim struggle of doing it. Shebib has said of this film more or less exactly what he's said of Pete and Joey: he wanted to make us *like* the revivalists, as people who buck the odds, whose belief in something transcends the laborious fact of their circumstances.

'The film that really shaped me was *Revival*,' he told me. 'Which nobody has ever seen, but won the Best Short at the Montreal Film Festival. Fuck, did that ever surprise me. Anyway, it's basically about fundamentalist Christians who preach on street corners. A lot of the film takes place on the corner of Queen and Spadina, and a lot in Allan Gardens, and it follows these very fundamental Christians. It was about this band of people, very working class, many of them English as I recall. This was 1963 when I shot it. I went for two or three occasions and I shot them, and then they were convinced that I had been chosen by God to come there and in the course of coming there I would be converted to their way of living.'[12]

He smiles. 'They were very sweet. There was this crazy, wacky guy preaching in Allan Gardens, and there would be crowds there making fun of him. To me it's the most fundamental film I've ever made because I believe in people's spirits. And the film makes fun of people. But not these people. It makes fun of the people making fun of them. That's what it's about.'

'I could make a film about people who believe that the earth is flat. So I made films about people on the outskirts of society which is what these people were. But the film itself was [a] tremendous leap forward in my filmmaking style. It was the direct predecessor of *Good Times Bad Times*.'[13]

Decades later, this impulse would be as strong a mechanism in Shebib's motivational apparatus as ever. When I interviewed him at length in 2011, he spoke with especially acute regret of the documentary he almost made for the NFB around 2005, but which was ultimately aborted – according to Shebib – due to institutional timidity: a portrait of the Communist Party in Canada. Once more, it wasn't the object of his subjects' devotion that appealed to the director but the devotion itself, the idealism that persisted despite the almost wholesale historical rejection of the cause.

'It got turned down and I was really pissed off,' Shebib said, 'because it would have been a wonderful, wonderful film about this group of people, the little engine that couldn't and never will and yet they still plough on.'

'They're surprisingly dedicated mom and pop people, not some Peter Lorre with a bomb under his arm. Dedicated Marxists, some of them professors, some of them working guys, all kinds of great characters, and what a wonderful documentary film this would have been. It's not about the history of the party, it's not a historical thing, though there might have been a little of that in it. It's about people tilting at windmills.'

'Whatever they believe in is irrelevant,' he stressed. 'I myself happen to be a Marxist. Unfortunately Marxism got a bad rap because it got started in the worst place in the world to get started in, which was Russia.'

'But that's irrelevant. Whether I believe in what they believe in is irrelevant. It's the people, their spirit, and striving for something they know they'll never win. They believe in the right to do it.'[14]

Basketball may at first seem exceptional in this regard. Until you realize it's not really about the team but its intensely unconventional and charismatic coach. Although engaged in an activity that by definition endorses conformity and the sublimation of individual personality, this is a man – still among the director's lifelong friends – who teaches nonconformity by example, and therefore eloquently represents Shebib's passionate interest in his 'people tilting at windmills.'

The culmination of this period was the deeply stirring *Good Times Bad Times*, a wrenching portrait of hospitalized and forgotten war vets. Shebib still considers it his greatest achievement, and it certainly represents the most eloquent attainment of the non-fiction filmmaker's balancing act of passion and objectivity. It also betokens his considerable respect for the past and those marooned there by an uncaring present.

Made at a time when there might not have been a less cool or sympathetic subject of a portrait than those who made war, *Good Times Bad Times* is therefore also a movie about the marginalized and misunderstood. The veterans in Shebib's film have become largely sidelined relics by the time of its making, but that only stimulates the filmmaker's intense affinity with their plight. If anything, it's a powerful statement against the uncaring frivolity of fashion and countercultural narcissism, an indictment of a collective memory that has forgotten the profound costs paid for the freedom that makes such forgetting possible.

As Peter Harcourt wrote in 'Men of Vision: Some Comments on the Work of Don Shebib' in 1976: 'The intricacies of this film could be studied in detail – the intricacies of the way it has been put together and those of its ultimate meaning. For who, finally, won the war? Certainly not the people who fought it, who experience the intense emotions of being at the front. Towards the end of the film we see an end-of-war rally in London and hear the legendary sound of Big Ben. Then, over shots of soldiers marching away, as so often in this film, the commentary draws upon lines from an extended poem by Joyce Cary, "Marching Soldiers," which he wrote at the end of the Second World War.'

'These lines are accompanied by the plaintive sounds of (Samuel) Barber's *Adagio*, creating a rich emotional effect difficult to describe – a fusion of exhilaration plus a sense of loss, a movement into accusation and uselessness.'[15]

This 'uselessness' is the real horror and tragedy in this film, the idea that these men, of all men, have become somehow redundant. It is this observation that Harcourt identifies as being central to Shebib's cinematic project: 'What are the qualities in life that hold people together, that might lead us collectively to a sense of identity or a feeling of purposefulness, a feeling of success? This is the question that, cumulatively, Shebib's films seem to ask.'[16]

Moreover, they ask it everywhere and of everyone, not simply of those who would seem to cohere to the filmmaker's own ideology and experience. For something of the same spirit is at work in *San Francisco Summer 1967*, a movie about the very generation that might otherwise be blamed for the casting off of the war vets. In this film, Shebib also sees a kind of striving for community on the margins, a retreat into communal ritual and the search for purposeful meaning in an increasingly dehumanizing world. Whether it's hippies, bikers, surfers, war vets, high school basketball coaches, street-corner fundamentalists, or, as we shall soon see, two displaced Maritimers in Toronto, the issue here is the struggle for dignity and decency and a sense of belonging, quests that for Don Shebib describe something essential in human experience. That the world people build only makes it harder for them to live happily within it is the irony that drives the engine of Shebib's art. It's the fuel that would take it, eventually and inevitably, on the road.

'The fact is,' Shebib told me, 'Pete and Joey are probably guys that I wouldn't want to spend the time of day with. But part of what drove me about *Goin' Down the Road* is I wanted to make a film about these two knuckleheads, and there's a direct line between Laurel and Hardy and Pete and Joey and Bob and Doug. Definitely between Bob and Doug McKenzie.'

'But I wanted it to be about these kinds of guys, show it to people who aren't from this world and have them *like* them.'[17]

Beginner's Licence

Shebib's documentary history would figure prominently in the delicately deft weaving of drama and social observation that is *Goin' Down the Road*. It's evident not only in the technique, which places actors in recognizably real contexts and records events with mobile, hand-held equipment, but also in the film's unsentimental but palpable respect for both its characters and their surroundings and its tacit acceptance of the integrity of the world it records, even if that world spurns the integrity of people like Pete and Joey. Implicit in this also is a respect for the viewer's integrity, our ability to make our minds up for ourselves, to appreciate these guys neither as misunderstood anti-heroes nor as pathetic victims but as people: guys just trying to get by in, as the Gene Pitney platter put it, 'a town without pity.'

Upon graduating from UCLA, Shebib returned to Toronto and cashed in on his non-fiction filmmaking skills. Largely under the auspices of CBC current affairs head Ross McLean, Shebib worked as both a documentary filmmaker and editor for the public broadcaster, which is where *Road* has its practical beginnings.

While working at the CBC current-affairs program *The Way It Is*, Shebib met and befriended a writer/editor named William Fruet and told him about an hour-long documentary he wanted to make. It concerned something Shebib had observed more than once growing up: what hap-

Allan Gardens, c. 1970. Courtesy of City of Toronto Archives, Fonds 124, file 2: f0124_fl0002_id0135.

pens when poor people from down east come to the city in search of employment and security, only to find they can't survive there either? He was thinking particularly about an unemployed cousin who'd come to stay with his family for a few weeks one summer years before, only to give up and return east when Toronto turned up nothing by way of a job.

Shebib's cousin was one of thousands. Throughout the 1960s, an estimated 150,000 Maritimers headed west in search of work, most of them ending up in Toronto. (When it came to selecting music for the 1982 SCTV parody of *Road*, Stompin' Tom Connors's 'To It and At It,' an ode to the travails of displaced Maritimers in Toronto, became the pitch-perfect theme.) Some found work, many more didn't, and their presence in the city functioned as a kind of underground of the displaced. The Maritimers converged in particular taverns and bars, moved to lower-rent neighbourhoods like Parkdale and Cabbagetown, and maintained their ties to home by singing along to bands and performers who specialized in down-east music. This was the community and phenomenon that Shebib wanted to make a non-fiction film about for the CBC. It was tentatively titled *The Maritimers.*

As he told Piers Handling, future CEO of the Toronto International Film Festival, in 1976: 'I wanted to make a film. It was to be an hour long documentary. In a way it was to be the kind of thing that Ralph Thomas eventually wound up doing. It was what they're doing now at the CBC in their *For the Record* series. Jack Winters at one time started to write the thing and it eventually didn't work out so I found another writer and he didn't work out.'

'Eventually I came across Bill Fruet who I was working with at the time anyway. He worked on *The Way It Is* as an editor. So then Bill wrote it. It was really based on an experience of my cousin on my father's side of the family – my father is from Cape Breton – who came up to Toronto when I was still in college and stayed with us for a month or so. It was in part just based on the problems he had existing. He ran into the same story as those guys down the line. The film was based upon that experience, of observing him.'[1]

Shebib had read a script based on a play Fruet had written called *Wedding in White* (to be filmed and directed by Fruet, featuring *Road*'s McGrath and Bradley, in 1972), and invited the writer to take a crack at a documentary about displaced Maritimers in the big city. As Fruet told me in 2011, 'I had written *Wedding in White* and I saw his documentaries and was very impressed. So we got talking, got to know each other and I gave him *Wedding in White* to look at, hoping he might like it because I thought he was very promising and I didn't think I had a chance in the world to ever become a director. He liked it very much – at least he said he did – because he asked me then if I'd be interested in this idea. And I just happened then to be working on a road idea myself. With two guys, but not like *Goin' Down the Road*. This would have probably been a lighter thing because when I was younger I was very impressed with shows like *Route 66*. That kind of thing. Anyway we got talking and he asked me [if] I'd be interested and I said "sure."'[2]

Fruet had come to Toronto from rural Alberta in the 1950s. He had hoped to gain work there as a writer, but his early years provided him with ample fodder to project onto the plight of Pete and Joey. Fruet ended up stacking pins in bowling alleys, sleeping in men's hostels, and spending a lot of time hanging desolately on the street, three activities he'd assign to his fictional creations. When the only vaguely writing-related job became open – as an obit writer for the *Globe and Mail* – the newspaper was deluged with literally hundreds of applications. By the time he and Shebib met, Fruet had succeeded in finishing a play. *Wedding in White* was a downbeat character study set in rural Alberta about a teenage girl who is forced to marry a much older man when she's raped and left pregnant by an army buddy of her brother.

Shebib liked the play, and was particularly impressed by Fruet's handling of character and dialogue. *The Maritimers* was intended to blend documentary and dramatic elements, so these skills would serve the project well. The men proceeded.

'We started going out to the places where these guys went,' Fruet told me. 'We drank with them, we really mixed it up with them. I really sort of caught their lingo and the interesting thing was, the experience that some of these people were going through was easy for me to draw on. I had gone through a lot of the same things myself when I came here. I came to go to school naively from the west and I thought I could get a job. I had studied theatre arts and I ended up working in bowling alleys. I ended up sleeping in flophouses. Everything you saw there. I didn't party as much because I couldn't drink beer, but that's what I could draw on.'

'I slept outside in January because I didn't have a place. I could understand what these guys were going through and I think it came quite easily. The bottling factory, same thing. It wasn't here, it was in another city, but I worked in a bottling factory.'[3]

It took some time. First of all, the CBC backed out when *The Way It Is* was cancelled in 1969. But Ross McLean had been impressed by Fruet and Shebib's work on the script, and told them they didn't need the broadcaster. He felt the story was strong enough to be re-conceived as a feature drama, and suggested they go and make a real movie of it. It was not like either of them had much to lose.

'It was only an hour,' Fruet said of the original made-for-TV concept, 'and it was very much still documentary, but with enough drama that Ross McLean said that "You should get this in the drama department. You should enlarge on it." So Don took it out and put it in there. And I re-wrote the script first to make it a feature, probably an hour and a half.'[4]

Originally, as Fruet told an interviewer in 1975, he imagined a story involving a young man's search for his alcoholic father, but that didn't seem to go anywhere. (Asked about this years later, Shebib didn't re-member this stage of conception.) Apart from Shebib's family history, Fruet's early Toronto experience, and the overwhelming fact of the massive migration of unemployed easterners to Toronto during the 1960s, fodder came, as Fruet told interviewer John Hofsess in 1975, from pubs and taverns. It would be in environments like this that much of *Road* would unfold.

'I went around in pubs and talked to Maritimers,' said Fruet in 2011. 'And once I found these two guys and realized halfway through our conversation that I was talking to Joey and Pete. The real McCoy. I lis-tened to these two guys for two hours, describing the flophouses they'd stayed in, and the *bugs*. Priceless stuff. It came so easy to write after that I didn't have to add much.'[5] Because Shebib knew where the Maritim-ers tended to hang out in Toronto, he and Fruet would go and simply sit and listen. They heard story upon story, and they took them all in. Fruet started writing.

With the script in shape, Shebib moved. On what exactly, he wasn't sure. Beyond making a movie, he had no plans. As he told Handling: 'The CBC backed out of the project and I never even considered a fea-ture – I just made this hour and half film. It was going to be a feature I guess but I never thought it would be shown anywhere. I never had any plans, any idea of what would happen to it.'[6]

As a wet-behind-the-ears operation functioning in a city with almost no tradition of local filmmaking, Shebib's production was guerrilla-style by necessity, and made up of hungry young would-be professionals, cu-rious acquaintances, and generous friends. To cast the movie, it was suggested Shebib contact Eli Rill, a former teacher at Lee Strasberg's Ac-tor's Studio in New York who had opened a nightly acting school above a strip joint – Le Strip Burlesque – on Yonge Street. A proponent of the 'method' school, Rill sent Shebib several actors, five of whom were appearing together in a play called *Soul and Molly B.* Among them were

Douglas McGrath, 34, Paul Bradley, 29, Jayne Eastwood, 23, and Cayle Chernin, 22. After auditioning them individually, Shebib hired them all, virtually casting all the lead roles – and a few of the small ones – for his movie in one fell swoop.

As Jayne Eastwood remembered in 2011, 'I don't know who heard about the audition first but we all ended up going. And we all nailed the part.' 'He liked our style of acting because it was very natural at the time,' she added. 'At that time in Toronto most of the opportunities were sort of at Shaw and the CBC and Stratford. And I think that time an English accent was rather in.'

'A more classical style of acting was popular at the time,' Eastwood said. 'Whereas we were kind of a more mumbling, naturalist, right out of the Actor's Studio sensibility. And it fit in well with what Don was doing because he was originally a documentary filmmaker. So a lot of his approach with this film had that kind of documentary, street style. And a lot of people actually thought that we were improvising when we did it but in fact it was very tightly scripted. That's why we got the movie.'[7]

It helped that McGrath, Bradley, and Eastwood all arrived in character and in costume – Eastwood especially resplendent in the prairie twister beehive she'd wear as Bets in the movie (and again in the 1982 SCTV take-off). But more important was the clear ability of Rill's students to seem almost effortlessly authentic. No borrowed mannerisms or boldly phoney accents. They looked the part of working-class street folk and they *seemed* it.

'I was at the auditions,' Fruet remember in 2011. 'I remember when Bradley and McGrath walked in. I couldn't believe it. It was them. Then they said they both had experience in the Maritimes. I remember thinking, "These are the guys. These *are* the guys. They're perfect."'[8]

As McGrath remembered years later, the teachings of Eli Rill and the circumstances of Shebib's script and audition meshed fortuitously. Both he and Bradley had had down-and-out experiences in their own

Doug McGrath, Paul Bradley, and Jayne Eastwood: Not Stratford.
Courtesy of Union Pictures.

lives, and Rill's process of excavating internal motivation allowed them to become Pete and Joey without resorting to much artifice.[9]

Bradley may have been the least experienced of the group professionally, but he was also the one who'd had the most challenging personal history. Raised by his mother in a downtown apartment, Bradley lived just a block or so away from McGrath near Allan Gardens, a public space that would become the setting of one of the film's most memorable improvised sequences.

Among his peers, Bradley was considered almost intimidatingly gifted: a natural mimic, inspired clown, and fearless improviser. But he was also a notoriously hard drinker, and his reliability for the purposes of a feature film was an open question. Of all the cast, he was the one Shebib was most worried about, but he was also the one the director was most impressed by. Decades later, Shebib would stand by his decision to hire Bradley as one of the most important he'd made – and the one that was most instrumental for the movie's emotional power. Shebib looks back on the casting of Bradley as one of the smartest moves of his career, and he almost didn't make it.

He remembered reading something about Cayle Chernin when the actress passed away in 2011, something about how he didn't want her for the movie. It wasn't true. 'There was a lot of stuff written about Cayle because of her death,' he told me. 'And Cayle was apparently thinking that maybe I wasn't that keen on her for the movie, and that I wanted somebody else, but it wasn't her that I wasn't keen on. The person I struggled with was Paul ... Because he really wasn't an actor, but he had that great face, so finally I bit the bullet and I said "I gotta go with him."'

'And it's a good thing I did because the film would have died without him,' Shebib explained. 'We would have been nowhere without him. I mean as good as Doug and Jayne and everybody else was, and as good as I was in terms of how I edited the film and how I made the film, he was the heart and soul of the film. So he was the one I agonized about.'[10]

Fruet remembers being awestruck by Bradley's gifts at least twice, and on both occasions by complete surprise. He remembers the night the crew was shooting Pete and Joey getting drunk in a tavern, and a bouncer marched up to quell the ruckus.

'It was in the bar scene, where they almost get into a fight,' says Fruet. 'Bradley just carries that scene, and it's not even written. He knows his timing, everything is there. You'd swear it was almost a scripted scene in a way to some degree. There are a few others that they took a little further than were written, and yet they spoke everything I wrote.'[11]

Then there's the scene, also set in a bar, where Pete tries to explain to Joey just how pointless their lives are. He uses the endless piling of empty crates as a metaphor, a crude kind of coming to political consciousness. 'In the script the scene's much shorter,' Fruet told me, 'and Don came to me a little after the film was made and he said "I want to enlarge this scene." It was based on a real incident I went through. I had had a job at a bottling plant and I remember this going through in my head: "Every day I'm packing the same *empty* cases. Nothing here to account for my work. For what I've done." And Paul's performance, sitting there listening to Pete like "What are you talking about?" It's beautiful, it's just beautiful.'

'I mean I wrote the lines,' Fruet adds, 'but he just brought it to a new level.'[12] What McGrath remembers about Bradley is how little he needed by way of actual teaching. 'I remember in the class,' he said, 'the thing that Eli said was that he couldn't say anything to him. He was a natural.'[13]

McGrath and Bradley lived very close together, and they'd hang out in Allan Gardens. They did so before they got hired for *Goin' Down the Road*, and they continued to do so throughout the shoot. 'We were all comfortable with each other, but Paul and I had time to work togeth-er,' said McGrath. 'And we basically worked the same. At the time Paul lived right on College Street in a hotel right beside Allan Gardens. I lived across the street up on Holmwood, a block away. So we hung out. Even read in the park. We would get the scenes and go through them. We improvised a little bit, but I think Fruet wrote some nice dialogue.'

'I really got to know him,' McGrath said of his friendship with Brad-ley. 'How he got to grow up and survived by his wits. He really survived by his wits. To get what he needed, to survive, he could con anybody.' Shrugging and smiling slightly, he added: 'I'm sorry we didn't work more together.'[14]

Just about everyone I spoke with said the same of Paul Bradley: how they wished they could have worked with and known him more, but how his personal problems made any deeper relationships almost im-possible. 'I would have liked him to have been more of a friend,' Mc-Grath told me in 2011, 'but I couldn't. Couldn't.'

'He had a lot of respect for me because of my history and so on but he never knew how much respect I had for him. And in a large sense that film rode on him and the friendship we established. He was so unique. I think it was Cayle that first said it, but I realized that Pete needed Joey more than he needed Pete. As I went along in life, I real-ized that to somehow follow this up should have been, would have been, part of my next work with him. But unfortunately that wasn't to happen.'[15]

'Paul Bradley was like a street guy,' Eastwood told me. 'He was really just a street guy. I don't know how he found out about Eli's workshop but he just found himself there. And he had us in hysterics. He was doing great stuff on stage. It was hilarious. It just completely opened a whole new world for Paul.'

'We were all really close,' said Eastwood. 'We were very, very close. It was the time too, you know what I mean? The '70s, really just coming out of the '60s, and I guess we felt like we had our own little Greenwich Village thing going on.'

'We definitely kind of hung out but Paul, god bless him, he just, um, he drank too much. Like he was even too wild for me and I was probably pretty wild in those days. I remember after the film I did *Godspell* and I ended up in Second City. I wasn't hanging out with Paul too much any more because the boozing was just like insane. Once he dropped in at my place and he wanted to come down and see me in Second City and I said "That's great, but I've got to go now, come on down when we do the improv set."'

'Well he had his vodka or whatever it was and he was sitting on my back porch and he said "Well that looks like a good mixer." He thought it was Hawaiian Punch. He actually mixed barbecue lighting fluid in with his vodka and he was so stoned by the time that he got to the theatre they had to throw him out because he was screaming at us on stage and everything. It was a sad end.'

'So the combination of being in that studio and then doing *Goin' Down the Road* kind of made him a star. But he kind of blew it, though, because he couldn't stop drinking.'[16] That was later. In the meantime, for Bradley and everyone involved, Don Shebib's movie felt like a long-overdue beginning.

By drawing his cast from Rill's students, Shebib was introducing another element of sympathetic outsider-ness to his production. As both McGrath and Eastwood remembered years later, Toronto was not exactly an accommodating place to performers who strayed from the conventional path of theatrical training. Which is to say, if you hadn't done Stratford or Shaw, and you didn't enunciate in the plummy tones of the mid-Atlantic, you weren't likely to find work.

At Rill's school, students were not only encouraged to practise a form of emotionally based performance derived from the method, they were heavily practised and tested in improvisation. While this kind of

Paul Bradley as Joey. Courtesy of Union Pictures.

training made them ideal for the quietly naturalistic performances required by Shebib – and would qualify Eastwood, for one, as a candidate for the inaugural Toronto Second City troupe – it put them decidedly on the outside of the English Canadian dramatic establishment. And it very likely provided them with a modicum of shared defensive energy that also synched seamlessly with their fictional counterparts. Whether or not he realized it at the time, by going to Rill's studio for his cast Shebib had found the perfect performers to play his 'losers.'

What Shebib did realize was that he'd found performers who wouldn't require much direction, and this perfectly suited his philosophy of what actors were supposed to do. As with John Ford and John Huston, who both insisted that the most important part of the casting process was finding people so right for the job the director was left free to tell the story as effectively as he could, Shebib settled on his cast because he knew he could trust them to do what he needed them to with as little guidance as possible. Under Rill's tutelage, Shebib's cast had already turned the soil.

'The classes were fabulous theatre,' wrote Cayle Chernin on the occasion of Paul Bradley's death in 2003, 'improvisations that grew and developed in front of our eyes, accompanied by sense memory and emotional memory exercises and always Eli cautioning us about our "sense of truth." He nurtured in us the Actors Studio dedication to re-creating life with truth and emotional clarity. Risking to be human and personal. Making choices.'[17]

With a cast almost entirely unknown and under-experienced – although Bradley had a long history as a carnival barker and fly-by-night huckster – it was precisely this unpolished rawness which lent the key roles a rare kind of authenticity. Moreover, Rill's tutelage encouraged his students' displays of unembellished naturalism. 'Eli had encouraged us to find ourselves and to stretch and find characters,' Chernin added. 'You can't judge your character; you must play the character with all the honesty and insight you can muster. He was adamant that indicating, exclaiming, technically executed manipulations of the audience's emotions were not our goal. Rather we were trying for a true exploration of a human being in an imaginary Set of Circumstances with a disciplined, responsive, open instrument with which we could "play" the drama of life in the ritual of Theatre, and in the immediacy, longevity and survival of Film – with spontaneity!'

'We must create credible life with an authenticity that belied the phoney traditional staginess that Canadian actors were often identified by at that time. Now when almost everyone is capable of being real on camera, it seems amazing that some of the first reviews thought *Goin' Down the Road* was a documentary, like some kind of pre-reality TV show that followed these God forsaken Canadian fools we know and love because they are loveable.'[18]

'Eli's methods were really based on improvising,' Eastwood recalled. 'Like we would just get up and basically he would give us a premise and we would just go. We would just improvise. There was a lot of discussion about "Don't hang signs out." You know what I mean? Don't play angry, you have to be angry. And that's the basis of the whole method acting really.'

'Obviously there is some pretend. You're projecting your emotions out there for an audience. It really like grounded us in a great reality. It was a very exciting workshop.'[19]

These guys certainly didn't look like movie stars, they didn't talk like movie stars, and they both looked like they'd had some hard times of their own. In the role of Bets, the waitress whom Joey makes pregnant and marries, Shebib cast Eastwood, who would become a staple figure in Canadian TV and movies (and who would brilliantly parody herself in the 1982 *SCTV* parody of *Road*), and twenty-two-year-old Chernin as Bets's friend Selina. The traffic-stopping pneumatic Nicole Morin was cast in the role of the Wilson pop factory's untouchably bodacious Nicole, and most of the remaining roles were played by available non-professionals. Practically no one in front of the camera had had much experience, and *Goin' Down the Road* is one instance where that was exactly what was required. One of the movie's most potent charms is the eerily naturalistic nature of the performances, especially as they mesh with the largely unscripted reality in which they perform.

In 2011, Shebib expressed his approach to casting the movie and directing his actors thusly: 'It's not that I stood back and let them do what they wanted. It's that I didn't, and still don't, know fuck all.'

'I don't know anything about acting,' he said. 'But I do know what's true. I mean, John Ford never said ten words to an actor in his whole fucking career. He is without a doubt the best Hollywood filmmaker ever. He never made a bad film. Ever. Not one bad movie.'

'He sat around and played poker with actors and bet with them or went to a ball game with them. But he didn't know anything about acting in that sense, and yet he instinctively knew a lot.'

'Directing films is *not* about directing actors,' Shebib explained. 'One of the things people in this country do not understand is that the difference between a television director and a real film director is that the film director is a storyteller. You have to look at the thing and say "Is there a story here?" Or find the story and mine it and understand it. Because if there's not a story in the script you've got to get one.'

'Anyway, John Ford says, "Your job is to tell the story, and if the story isn't good fix it." People think it's directing the actors. Directing the actors on a feature film should occupy about 15 per cent of the director's job.'[20] With Rill's alumni association; he more than got that 15 per cent covered, and he was free to get on with the business of telling the story.

With a start-up fund of $19,000, which Shebib was granted by the freshly launched Canadian Film Development Corporation (since renamed Telefilm Canada), *Goin' Down the Road* went into production in the summer of 1969. It was not a seamless affair. Shebib's original hopes to shoot the movie in 35 mm were dashed by budgetary restrictions, and on more than one occasion money ran out or the director had to go scrounging for stock the night before a scene was scheduled to be shot. A grocery cart doubled as a camera dolly, the uninsured hundred-buck jalopy (with 'My Nova Scotia Home' emblazoned in flames by Carroll Ballard on the side) doubled as both character and crew transportation, and everyone had to be prepared to shoot at any time circumstances presented themselves favourably. Indeed, some of the movie's most memorable scenes, like Joey and Bets's legion hall wedding, the boys delivering flyers in a leafy October snowstorm, and the spontaneous singalong at Allan Gardens, were all the result of serendipity.

'For us that was very exciting,' Eastwood explained in 2011. 'And we were young. I didn't even expect it to be any other way. We didn't know that trailers existed or craft service or drivers or full lunches for the crew. This was our first film. We thought that's the way you shoot a film. It didn't seem odd to us.'

'It just seemed like a grand adventure. We were just ready and willing at all times to do the best we could. And it felt like we were all in it together because it was a really small crew, right? I mean there was no crew. Jim McCarthy was on sound, I think he did the lighting as well, directed by Richard Leiterman of course. And Shebib. That's it. *That's it.* It really was almost just like running around Toronto with a camera.'

'We were all on the same page, so it was really easy to do. And we loved the whole kind of sort of guerrilla shooting. Like we were really kind of into being in Allan Gardens, like when Paul and Doug and I are completely almost on the street and just being part of those street people. That's the kind of stuff we just thought was really cool. It's still cool today. It's a good way to shoot a film, really.'[21]

For no one were these circumstances more perfect than cinematographer Richard Leiterman, the most experienced member of the crew besides Shebib. At thirty-five, Leiterman was already a pre-eminent practitioner of the vérité school of shooting. Beginning with his work as a CBC cameraman, followed by a long collaborative stint with Allan King (Leiterman shot King's fly-on-the-wall landmark *A Married Couple*), and as cameraman to Frederick Wiseman on the widely heralded *High School*, Leiterman knew how to work quickly, cheaply, and effectively. Moreover, as a documentary veteran he shared a certain intuitive sensibility with Shebib, an instinct for capturing exactly the detail – in a face, a gesture, a passerby, or a glass of beer on a table – that spoke the volumes the characters couldn't.

Road was Leiterman's first foray into fiction. Another of the crew's outsiders, Leiterman had spent years as a garbage collector, a truck driver, and – as more than one of his biographies stresses – a beachcomber. Partly self-taught as a cameraman, Leiterman had spent his long apprenticeship to Allan King learning how to shoot under stressful and uncontrollable conditions. In one of his most famous stunts, for the film *Will the Real Norman Mailer Please Stand Up?*, he had followed the notoriously bluster-prone author to the front of the police lines at an anti-war demonstration in Washington. Anticipating Mailer's next move, Leiterman stepped across the line and swung his camera in order to film what he sensed was going to happen next.

'I thought this is the only way to show them crossing,' Leiterman told an interviewer in 2002. 'Mailer spotted me and said, "Okay you guys, I'm going." Off he went across the line, and I was there walking backwards as he did. The police tried to stop us. They asked us where we thought we were going, and Mailer said, "I'm transgressing the police lines." And they said, "Well, you're not supposed to do this." Meanwhile, I'm still shooting. I don't know how far we got, about a hundred yards, when the police finally collared Mailer and said, "That's as far as you're going, Mr. Mailer. We don't care who you are." I captured most of this on film. As they carted him off, they were going to cart me off too.'[22]

The line crossed was more than the not-so-thin blue one in front of the Pentagon. By stepping in front of his subject under those conditions, Leiterman might also have been directing Mailer, coaxing him to make a move. The cinematographer was acting on intuition: sensing not only what might happen next, but for the purposes of drama, what *needed* to happen next. And it did.

Whatever the motivation, the act endeared the cameraman to the combative writer, who spoke fondly of Leiterman's calming presence in his book *Armies of the Night*. 'The next day,' wrote Mailer in his intermittent third-person mode, 'Mailer had the opportunity to watch Leiterman at work. Whenever he saw Mailer he would smile. This would seem part of his photographic technique. He would always smile encouragingly at his subject. After a while one was glad to see him.'[23]

This knack for putting his subjects at ease, even under the most uneasy conditions, became a hallmark of the Leiterman style. But the trust he established extended both ways: both in front and behind the camera. When filming *A Married Couple*, which required Leiterman to literally live in the home of a Toronto couple whose marriage would dissolve before the scrutiny of Leiterman's lens, he was sufficiently unobtrusive not only to allow Billy and Antoinette Edwards to be completely and sometimes wincingly themselves, but to make King himself superfluous. After spending a few days with the crew in the house, the director realized he didn't need to be there at all.

'For the first three or four weeks I was around the house a lot,' King said in 1971. 'Later, I found it worked best for me to stay away. A director in that sort of situation is a bit irrelevant. You need enough time to observe a lot of things and you drop in; but there is no need. I find for me at any rate, to stand and tell a cameraman "point here, point there, turn on here, turn off there." All you really do is interfere.'[24]

Left to his own instincts, Leiterman was providing King with exactly what he wanted and needed. Indeed, it was almost like having an extension of himself in the house. A proxy director. 'In the end I very specifically gave Richard a credit as associate director,' King told Alan Rosenthal in 1971, 'because the contribution that he made to the filming was so very, very important. There was no way of doing that kind of a film without an exceptional person shooting, because he had to make the basic choices of when he was going to shoot and when not. We talked a lot about strategy and something about tactics as we were working, but often it was the choice that Richard made; in a very real sense he is the Associate Director.'[25]

Knowing he was going to be making his first feature film under almost entirely unpredictable circumstances, Shebib chose his cameraman the way he selected his cast, by asking who would need the *least* amount of direction? Who could be called upon to not only function but maybe thrive when the unforeseen erupted?

'*Goin' Down the Road* was probably a picnic for Richard but he just knew what to do,' Jayne Eastwood said in 2011. 'Of course I don't know anything about camerawork but I thought he was amazing. We all really looked up to him.'[26]

Many years after he performed as Pete McGraw in front of Leiterman's camera, McGrath spoke with lingering amazement at the cinematographer's calm, quiet, imperturbable efficiency. He remembers waiting for Leiterman's subtle gestures to indicate when he should turn, when he should stand still, when he was doing absolutely the right thing. 'Leiterman was my focus,' McGrath told me in 2011. 'He would say "Look here, on the edge here." I would follow him backwards along a cliff because I trusted him.'[27]

As did Shebib, who conferred constantly with Leiterman concerning camera set-ups, moves, and how to get the best possible image from often brutally ill-lit settings. Often, these discussions were spur-of-the-moment affairs. Literally, the two men were figuring out the best way to shoot the movie as they went along. It might have had a script, story, and actors in the beginning and the end, but in between – in the actual assembly – *Goin' Down the Road* felt powerfully akin to a documentary.

'Don also came from a documentary background,' Leiterman said in 2002, 'and we were both trying things out when we did *Goin' Down the Road*. Who knew if we really knew what we were doing? But it worked beautifully because it was fresh, and we were fresh. We had no rules. We didn't know any rules. It was a trial by fire, the beginning of something different.'[28]

As both Leiterman (who died in 2005) and Shebib have pointed out, theirs was a collaboration that almost instantly resulted in a bond of trust: Shebib would block a scene, let it play, and leave Leiterman to capture the most significant elements as it played out. This is evident in the film's much-heralded use of close-ups, incidental background details, and moments of quiet, contemplative reaction, most of which are the result of Leiterman's vérité-steeped shooting style. Sometimes, the texture of apparent reality captured by the film so effectively blurred generic borders that *Goin' Down the Road* was frequently referred to as 'documentary drama.'

'We'd discuss the scene, then we'd block it out, and then I'd suggest a camera position,' Leiterman told Alison Reid and Peter Evanchuk in 1978. 'If he didn't like it, he'd propose an alternative. I think the camera positions were as much my work as his. It was a very free thing – he'd hired me to do the camerawork and he pretty much left me alone.'

'He always likes to take a squint through. He was a cameraman himself.'[29]

If not quite guerrilla filmmaking, the shooting method for *Goin' Down the Road* was certainly an exercise in urban jungle survivalism. To make a movie in Toronto in those days (and not many were) it was simply a matter of going out and doing it: there were no film offices to obtain permissions from, no location shooting protocols to follow, no real history of local filmmaking, period. (The movie contains a few instances of passersby checking out the actors and crew, which only adds to the sense of real life taking its course.)

This meant that many sequences designed to be shot in particular settings were ultimately shot in what was available. If Shebib wanted a scene in a restaurant or bar, he'd go in and ask if he could bring his crew in for fifteen minutes or so. Or they'd simply go in and shoot, hoping they'd have enough time to get something printable before being asked to leave. When it came to shooting Joey and Bets's wedding in the legion hall, the booze was plentiful but the extras scarce, so Paul Bradley (already a method-appropriate few brews in, according to Shebib) simply went out to the street and lured people in with the promise of free beer.

'It was fun,' McGrath said over forty years later. 'I mean here we were in a feature film. We weren't getting any money, but we knew each other and we were having a great time. I mean we're not twenty-one any more, we're twenty-nine, thirty but we had an incredible good time. Then Don would call and go "Doug it's raining! We've got to go and get this!" I remember I saw these kids in the park and said "Can you go and get your group together and come back?" So we just went down there and improvised with them.'

'That's partly the documentary sense that Don probably has,' McGrath said. 'He had us. We were working on the real, the natural, what we call method.'

'We called Don "The Bear,"' McGrath added. 'The one thing that I do remember, because of the freedom that we had is that Don had not worked with actors before. So he didn't know what not to do and he didn't interfere. There was some discussion with him, but at one point he said "Let 'em work," and he did. Because he didn't not know what to do. It was his very first film with actors, so he lucked out too.'[30]

Fruet hung around the production as frequently as possible, drinking in the spectacle of his words becoming dialogue in a real, honest-

Yonge Street, ca. 1969: The set. Courtesy of City of Toronto Archives, Fonds 200, series 1465, file 312: s1465_fl0312_it0061.

to-god movie. He remembers marvelling at how gracefully the script seemed to flow from the page to the mouths of the cast, how intuitively Leiterman and Shebib seemed to click, and how adroit the director was at adapting to whatever situation presented itself. Quickly, he also learned not to bother Shebib with anything by way of unwanted suggestions. Fruet wanted to become a director and Shebib knew he wanted to become a director, but this wasn't Fruet's movie to direct. Laughing about it more than forty years later, Fruet remembers Shebib deliberately providing him with bogus shooting locations to keep the writer away from the set.[31]

Perhaps the most poignant scene in the movie is the spontaneous singalong McGrath refers to that takes place in Allan Gardens. Pete, Joey, and Bets are on the serious outs by this time, and the motley congregation of bottle-sharing street folk gathered around a guitar-playing country singer provides a potent metaphor for the sad strength of marginalized communities: united by circumstance, music – the song, unscripted and uncannily perfect, is 'Sing Me Back Home' – and booze, and temporarily enjoying something like family under a cold, grey Toronto sky. The moment ends when a tussle over a bottle results in a shattered mess and people instantly disperse, the fleeting moment gone like leaves in an autumn wind.

It's one of finest instances of vérité-style filmmaking found anywhere, and it only happened because Shebib heard and saw the gathering in Allan Gardens that day and ran to a pay phone to get anyone who was available for the scene. Had he not been there, or had the camera and actors not arrived in time – had he not had a dime – one of *Goin' Down the Road*'s most eloquent sequences might never have been filmed.

A similar miracle occurred on the morning the crew was shooting the sequence where Joey, Pete, and Bets – now unemployed and almost completely broke – move into the decrepit Cabbagetown rooming house after being evicted from their high-rise. As they filmed the group carrying boxes up the stairs to the urine-scented room the three of them will share, a uniformed cop passed them on his way down. It's hard to imagine a single image that says more about the unforgiving plight of the underprivileged in Toronto in 1969 than that silent shadow of authority moving through the corridor.

Accidents, happenstance, and pure necessity were constantly conspiring in the crew's favour. In the sequence where Pete and Joey are whooping it up in a Yonge Street tavern frequented by Maritime expats, they're approached by a bouncer – a real one – insisting the boys tone down their language or leave. 'Great tunderin' *Jaysus*,' brays Bradley in response. 'What's wrong wit' *Jaysus*?' Another real-life reminder of the boys' status as undesirable urban aliens.

One day in October 1969 the city was hit with a sudden freak snowstorm, blanketing the still-green trees and grass in fresh white powder. Seizing a photogenically irresistible moment, Shebib called the crew to shoot a sequence of Pete and Joey delivering flyers door to door and horsing around in the snow. Shebib cut the scene, utterly unplanned and unscripted, into the film's near-final act. The result – of both the visual splendour and the narrative placement – lends an especially pungent poignancy to the drama. By showing up just prior to the final crash of hopes and dreams, the sudden snow comes to represent a symbolic expression of Pete and Joey's lost but lingering boyish idealism, the persistence of which only makes the bleakness of their plight that much more ominously foreordained.

After shooting for eight weeks, Shebib's tiny budget was exhausted. By that time, however, he was beginning to think of his movie as something other than a personal project. For the first time, he imagined he might actually be making something special, or at least something someone else might be willing to watch. For the first time, he was driven to get the thing finished and, just maybe, released.

If Shebib had demonstrated a certain beginner's reticence in the actual shooting of *Goin' Down the Road* – allowing generous creative space for Leiterman and his cast – in the editing he was in full command, and *Goin' Down the Road* is nothing if not a commandingly well-cut movie. On the commentary track of the 2002 DVD release, Shebib speaks of his need to stretch out the film in the editing – and how he'd kept shooting hundred-foot rolls of city footage long after principal production – yet another example of how necessity became one of the *Road*'s most powerful and eloquent expressive allies.

Consider, for example, the role of montage sequences in the movie. On the one hand, they are legion: it seems that for every scene or two of spoken dialogue there's a montage sequence set to music, that almost every instance of dramatic action is followed by a pause for reflection, wordlessness, and the distilled observation of character in environment. Shebib might have intended stretching, but the result is deepening. Not only do the montage sequences function evocatively as forms of purely cinematic interlude, they are thoroughly appropriate and fundamental to the narrative. For one thing, this is a story of people to whom not much happens – that's their tragedy – and for whom words don't come easily. The many montage sequences therefore capture not only this state of suspended anticipation and enforced paralysis, they tell us much about the inner lives of these quietly enduring souls. Far from stretching the drama or padding it, they become it. The repeated spectacle, for instance, of Pete's chilly wanderings on Toronto's streets is a form of its own soliloquy. The film's generous use of montages might have been motivated by Shebib's practical concerns that the story needed padding, but the padding became essential. While Shebib might not have realized it at the time, his movie *needed* the interludes to be properly told. But to be told quite so effectively and economically, it also needed an editor of uncommon skills. Here, as in other matters, Don Shebib was challenged by circumstance into something special. Unlike his characters, his film was getting somewhere.

'There was no conscious design in what I wrote whatsoever,' Shebib said in 1976. 'I had made no distribution agreements or anything until I got the film finally together and then I said "Gee! Maybe I can find someone who'd like to screen the film."' By that time, *Goin' Down the Road* was a film I really wanted to make most of all.'[32]

Shebib called Bennet Fode, a distributor and exhibitor who operated the New Yorker theatre on Yonge Street. Deeply impressed by what he saw – which included numerous glimpses of the street right outside his office doors – Fode agreed to help finance the completion of *Goin' Down the Road* in exchange for the right to the film's premiere and first run. For his part, the offer left Shebib stunned. For it hinted at something he had never considered: a successful movie. 'All I ever wanted was a screening,' he said to me. 'Just one screening. So I could see it with an audience and see how it was gonna work.'

'And I didn't know anything about distribution. If it wasn't for Bennet Fode seeing the film and saying "I want to distribute it," who knows? I almost dropped dead. I said "Holy Christ." I mean I didn't really know what was going on at the time.'[33]

With the money provided by Fode, Shebib was able to blow up his 16-mm movie to 35 mm, another key factor in the film's final texture of vérité docu-dramatic realism. On a big screen, *Road* looked raw, grainy, and captured on-the-fly, which no doubt accounted for the fact, recalled by Cayle Chernin and several others, that many who saw it thought they were actually watching the documentary that Shebib had originally intended.

For years afterward, McGrath found himself disabusing people of exactly that: he'd have to tell them that the film *wasn't* a documentary, and that what they'd been watching was in fact an honest-to-pete movie. 'When we were promoting it, somehow somebody said – or maybe

Don said – that he had picked these guys up on the street,' McGrath told me. 'In fact I remember in Calgary some guy said "He just picked you guys up on the street, right?" I couldn't believe it. So I said "No, the difference between me and Pete is that Pete's on his way down the road. I'm an actor with a successful film on my hands. That's the difference."'[34]

The other benefit added by the blow-up's facsimile of almost journalistic observation was the mediating of the movie's more melodramatic, if not to say credibility-straining, elements. Because the film is so effectively immersed in a kind of unfettered realism and apparent spontaneity, it's much easier to accept certain developments – like Pete's profoundly naive interview with an advertising company ('Back home I watched a lot of commercials on TV'), Joey's reckless credit spending on his new apartment, or Nicole's otherwise utterly unaccountable agreement to let Pete take her out on a date – on a kind of formal faith. The movie's style, in other words, goes a long way to selling its content.

And so it came to pass that *Goin' Down the Road*, a movie at least partly about dreams dying on Yonge Street, actually opened there on 2 July 1970.

The Road Rolls

On screen, the road tilts downward from Cape Breton, courtesy of stock images that appear beneath the then barely known folksinger Bruce Cockburn's plaintive title song. (Which Cockburn, to the apparent deep disappointment of Shebib, never permitted to be released on a soundtrack on the basis that the words – yearning, hopeful, and laced with lonesome idealism – weren't his but the characters'.)[1] The pictures are sad: sun reflects harshly on still waterways, children play on gravelled streets, hulks of fishing trawlers lay abandoned, forsaken people with sunken faces. A good place to leave behind, surely, but the kind that sticks in the souls of those who do.

This probably accounts for the bounce in Joey's step as he slings his gear in the back of his gaudily flame-painted convertible Impala, with barely a look back at the mother of whom a word will never again be spoken. Her posture in front of the house is implacably solemn, a Walker Evans attitude, as though this is a departure that warrants no impression. The sun is already tilting over the landscape (Etobicoke now standing in for Nova Scotia), so it's either early in the morning or approaching evening. Either way, the light seems already to be draining away.

Pete is waiting alone by the side of the road, windbreaker over his T-shirted shoulder, bag in the gravel. There's no home or mother he's

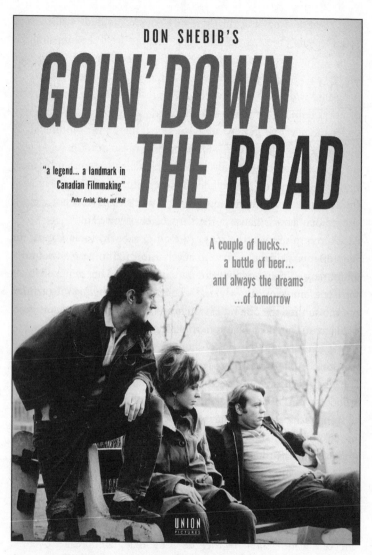

DON SHEBIB'S

GOIN' DOWN THE ROAD

"a legend... a landmark in Canadian Filmmaking"
Peter Feniak, Globe and Mail

A couple of bucks...
a bottle of beer...
and always the dreams
...of tomorrow

UNION
PICTURES

An accidental classic is born. Courtesy of Union Pictures.

seen to be leaving, and this state of elemental solitude will become Pete McGraw's most consistent visual context: we'll see him similarly alone and outside throughout the film – a spectator even in his own movie – and he'll come to strike us as someone who's doomed never to hang that windbreaker up for long. This makes Pete the embodiment of an existential state as well as a dedicated wanderer. He stands for that which can never be attained, and that's what this movie is ultimately all about: the soul made restless for something it can never have. At least Joey leaves a home and family behind, which may account for his more buoyant, dependent, and childlike nature. Pete, who bears the movie's burden of disappointment as well as dramatic emphasis, is only doubly driven for anchor because he's never seen to have had it.

Once on the road, the music kicks into a honky-tonkier gear, the boys start yanking playfully on Joey's rubber-kitty rear-view mirror adornment, flinging drained stubbies in the ditch and generally making like a couple of guys who really believe they're driving into a different movie than the one we're watching – which began on such a note of abject melancholy. As if to remind them – and this abrupt braking from high-gear hopes to gravel-shoulder reality will also strike a recurring note – the boys are next seen attending to a flat in the still-setting sunlight. But it isn't just the tire that's leaking. So are Joey's spirits. He wonders whether or not they've made the right choice, prompting Pete to stop plucking on the guitar while Joey pumps the tube.

'Listen Joey. It's gonna be so different. There you can get all kinds of jobs. Not just sweat and dirt all the time.'

This re-sparks Joey's optimism, never mind that he's the one sweating in the dirt at the moment: 'When we get us some money,' he says, tire-iron in hand like a wand, 'We'll get us a place in one of them fancy apartment buildings, with a swimming pool and broads everywhere, eh?'

They arrive in Toronto in high spirits, descending from the Don

Valley Parkway with a cocky warning to the city's parents: 'Hide your daughters and lock your doors!'[2]

The city obliges. Everything, from this moment on, will be locked up tight as far as Pete and Joey are concerned. One of our first glimpses of Pete and Joey arrived in Toronto is through the window of a Scarborough house whose curtains are closed so the inhabitants can hide inside. They're an aunt and uncle of Pete's – and therefore the movie's only suggestion of his family – who are horrified to have these rube Maritimers blown up on their front step. When the curtain closes and the boys wander off, Pete's aunt and uncle will disappear.

The boys are at a phone booth, calling an old Cape Breton buddy named Hanson about those jobs Pete is convinced grow on trees out here. He's doing his best to remain chipper as the unheard news gets inevitably worse, and Joey looks through the glass with his patented expression of canine anticipation. There are no jobs, Pete reports to Joey, and Hanson hasn't got any room to put them up for the night.

In the Salvation Army men's hostel, Joey lies on the upper bunk drinking in the atmosphere of seedy, rusty-springed despair. Pete's reading the classified section of a newspaper, keeping his optimism up even as Shebib's cutaways – to the sunken, hope-drained faces of the men in the nearby bunks – intimate once again the folly of it all. They're not the first guys to come in here with disposable dreams, and they might well live to look back on younger versions of themselves arriving late some night several years on. In the meantime, however, Pete's seen the *real* Toronto, the one he always knew was here, the one just waiting for him and Joey to come along and chug their fill of. It's right there in the want ads: 'Listen to this: "reservation agents, textile salesman, assistant manager, sales trainees ... We offer excellent promotional opportunities for the right man." Or listen to this: "Management trainer, large advertising company has opening for young man interested in the advertising ...."'

Toronto from the air, ca. 1970: The forbidding city. Courtesy of City of Toronto Archives, Fonds 124, file 2: f0124_fl0002_id0021.

Pete flops back on the bed, as though flung there by the sheer force of future brightness. 'Now *this* is more like it,' he says, patting his chest contentedly. 'It's all right here. All you gotta do is go out and get it! What's wrong with that Hanson?' Momentarily at least, the boys are re-delivered to dreamland, cheerfully oblivious to those possible projections of their own future perched mutely on the cots around them.

The next day, Pete is alone on the street, as happy and hopeful as we'll ever see him. He's wearing a windbreaker with a necktie, brimming with confidence (which we already know is probably unwarranted). He checks out the tall buildings and bustling pedestrians that stream by, and enters a door. We cut to him strutting somewhat self-consciously between a row of office desks, the windbreaker-tie combo giving away his uneasy intrusion on this setting. And we are set up for one of the movie's most indelible scenes.

Pete is asked by the man – glasses, shirtsleeves, distracted – sitting across the desk from him just what on earth possessed him to think he could get a job as an advertising executive? Pete's answer is both perfectly reasonable and almost wincingly ridiculous, a burst of naive, utterly guileless honesty that I remember squirming through even when I first saw the movie at age thirteen. Pete has decided that he'd like to get into advertising because he's *always* been into advertising. Back home, as he explains, he used to watch commercials all the time and always enjoyed them. Especially the car commercials.

The personnel man, whose motivation for even letting this guy into his office is suspicious, basically informs Pete that he's out of his mind. There's more to making TV commercials than simply watching and enjoying them – though Pete never learns precisely what – and it takes a college degree to acquire this secret knowledge anyway. The executive then takes a call, announces rather too loudly that he doesn't expect he'll be tied up much longer, and the interview is over.[3]

When next we see Pete, he's in a diner late at night. (These public spaces – taverns, greasy spoons, record stores, etc. – are Pete and Joey's most habitual urban element. They make their most momentous decisions in them, exchange their most dramatic news, ponder their plight, and generally abide in the absence of any stable domestic environment. They are spaces also replete with the faces of real people caught there, and thus thicken the texture of incidental actuality.)

Joey sneaks up and surprises Pete, exuding the kind of infantile bonhomie that's his stock-in-trade. Pete explains the advertising career is a non-starter ('I didn't see anything I liked'), but Joey waves it off. He knows a guy who can get them both jobs at a bottling factory, starting the next day. Pete deflates a little, but it's a job.

Shebib's bottling-plant montage instantly conveys bleak industry and ceaseless, rattling noise. The boys are seen working full-out from the get-go, surrounded by people who emanate a stale aura of downsized dreams. They don't know it yet, but this is as good as it will get for Pete and Joey, and it doesn't look too good.

First paycheques in pocket, the boys bolt out into the parking lot and into the night. The music kicks into up-tempo overdrive, the neon lights burst the night, and the factory boys are loose. It's Yonge Street time.

Shot at night on 16 mm, Toronto's most famous strip looks less like a beckoning urban glitter-dome than an underground corridor lit with random torches of possibility and temptation. The darkness bears down from above and at the edges, and the boys sprint through it sporting up girls – none game to play – laughing heartily, and hitting A&A's, the long-closed, late-houred, multi-levelled record store that used to sit right next to Sam the Record Man near the teeming hub of Yonge and Dundas. It was a good place to go and blow what was left of a paycheque, scope girls, or kill time until a show started. Pete, Joey, and the pop-bottle boys pour in.

A vision crosses Pete's sightline. She's ethereally beautiful, in a deli-

Yonge Street, ca. 1969: The boulevard of broken dreams. Courtesy of City of Toronto Archives, Fonds 200, series 1465, file 312: s1465_fl0312_it0054.

cate, fine-featured, straight-haired, Emmylou Harris kind of way. Appropriately, she seems to float upward towards the classical section, Pete following like a thunderstruck teenager. Upstairs, where it's so much quieter he might have entered another dimension, he pretends to be flipping through the stacks. She's listening to Satie's *Trois Gymnopédies* on the turntable, and Pete makes his move.

An instant bust. Although she indulges his attempts to appeal to their 'shared' musical interests with a smile, she quickly turns on her heel and resumes floating out of his reach. After clumsily knocking the needle across the grooves, Pete asks the clerk for the name of the composer and buys the record, tucking it under his arm and heading out to the sidewalk with the lads. They show each other the country-and-western booty they've purchased or cadged, and the night ends with the bunch listening to a Maritime band sing about wanting to be back home. The Satie record is presumably tucked somewhere beneath a wooden tavern chair, waiting for its own moment to evoke something else that's not there. The Yonge Street Friday night is over.

So quickly are they back at the factory you'd think Monday arrives right after last call Friday. They're still horny. When Nicole (Nicole Morin), the factory's other work-stopping siren, comes bobbing across the floor, the guys make like howling, lust-smacked wolves in a Tex Avery cartoon. (Joey, not surprisingly, delivers the best horn-dog impression.) Nicole has what all the guys want – none more so than Pete – but only reports directly to the factory foreman 'Frenchy.' Indeed, as if to emphasize the two-solitudes nature of the abyss separating the boys who stack crates and the stacked boss's assistant, we're told that Nicole, too, is French. 'Is she *ever*,' growls Pete.

So quickly does the pace of incident quicken in this middle section of *Road*, the sensation is like the out-of-control clarity that precedes a car crash. Women figure prominently. They mark the critical point where desire has a nasty way of giving way to disaster – at least for boys like these two – and where giddy Friday nights really do seem to slam right into grim Monday mornings.

Joey has met a waitress whom he takes Pete to watch through the window of the diner where she works. (It's a cinch imagining Joey talking her up there, over coffee after last call.) Pete's not keen – Betty is no Nicole – but he indulges his friend's offer of a double date with Betty's friend Selena. 'Why not?' he shrugs.

In the car, the girls eat fries and talk shop to Pete's evident disdain. They probably strike him as stupid, but we know there's more to it than that: Betty and Selena, who if anything are touching in their eager acceptance of these two pop-bottle jockeys living in an apartment wallpapered with boobs-out girlie mag pinups, are too perfectly suited to their dates. They're precisely the kind of girls one would expect Pete and Joey to be sitting and eating French fries with in a flame-painted convertible, and as such mark a surrender, a surrender to what was left behind. For Pete, they're failure in fresh perms.

The couples are seen in a montage sequence. Ostensibly, everybody's having a good time: the guys walking busy streets with arms around their dates, laughing, goofing off at the Scarborough Bluffs. They drive the big convertible to the posh streets of Rosedale, where they look as out of place as escaped zoo animals. Pete sees his future there, but his companions dismiss the idea as ridiculous. Next morning, Pete refuses to get out of bed for work, as he's apparently set his sights on higher goals. Selena is a dead end. 'All that dumb Selena does is talk,' he complains to Joey. 'Last night, she told me about her old lady, her brother's hernia operation, and Christ knows what.'

'What I need is somebody like that Nicole,' he says, squeezing his pillow. 'If I had that dame in bed here right now ...'

Joey leaves. Reality check. Pete accepts his fate and turns up at the factory, where the crates ceaselessly clatter their cargos of soda pop. It's unbearable.

Later, in a scene inspiringly re-situated by Shebib from the factory lunchroom to a tavern, Pete explains to Joey the way of the world.[4] Tallying the number of pop crates they've stacked every hour and every day since they started, he arrives at a bleak conclusion: 'Okay, now get this. That's twelve every minute, seven hundred and twenty an hour, five thousand seven hundred and sixty in a day. Which means that in the two months we've been here, we've piled two hundred and thirty thousand, four hundred crates. *Each*!'

Pete is trying to make a point about the utter existential pointlessness of it all – 'Can't you see there ain't nothing happening? That everything keeps going around in the same stupid circles doing the same stupid thing over and over? And there ain't nothing happening?' – but Joey is clueless. He's in a tavern with his best buddy drinking beer paid for by money provided by this 'pointless' job. What's Pete's problem?

Pete makes a last stab at clarity before giving up and downing his glass. Joey still doesn't get it. 'I want just to do something that matters, something that shows for myself. Says I was there.' He holds his hands up as though regarding a sign: 'Peter McGraw was there.' Joey's at a complete loss. 'Pete, you'll never change. You'll never change. Why don't you give up all these big ideas?'

It's time to act. At the lunch room, the factory guys are playing cards with a nudie deck, and Pete announces he's going to make a move on Nicole. Although only Joey has enough faith in his buddy to bet a fin on him, everyone's pleased when Pete swaggers from the pop machine with the news: he has a date to climb the Alps.

(In credibility-teasing terms, this rivals the advertising agency interview. Why would the knockout wolf-bait Nicole possibly agree to go out with such a no-name-brand hoser like Pete – who has already demonstrated his manly poise by driving a forklift into a pile of crates by way of impressing her – unless it was to fulfil some kind of cruel dramatic destiny? Is she a secret agent for the Department of Class Containment?)

Pete and Joey add it up: 'Can't you see there ain't nothing happening?'
Courtesy of Union Pictures.

Appreciating the stakes of the event, the boys take Pete out on a spruce-up spree, which only ratchets our dread up accordingly. Anticipation in this movie tends to rise in direct proportion to humiliation, and levels now rise to embankment-busting heights. To make matters worse, the lads trail along behind Pete on date night, hanging out the convertible like barking dogs on their way to a run in the park.

It's bad, every bit as bad as we feared. Nicole has suggested going dancing, and so she does, though not with Pete. In what may be the movie's single most dubiously economical moment of cinematographic inspiration, new meaning is given to the term 'rack focus' as Richard Leiterman shifts in a single shot from the foreground spectacle of Nicole's stupendous breasts in full, swinging, Friday night dance-floor fury to Pete watching miserably from a table in the distance. It is hard to imagine when looking and touching have ever seemed so far apart.[5]

At her apartment, Pete follows Nicole desperately up the stairwell. The carload of canines is parked across the street. Without so much as looking back, Nicole blows Peter off with some lame excuse about a visiting girlfriend and closes the door on his face. Her job is done, Pete's humiliation is utter, and we never see Nicole again. Pathetically, Pete ducks in the shadows of the stairwell until the dogs have been called off.

It's a beautiful day, presumably the Saturday following the Friday night horrors. Pete, Joey, Bets, and Selena are on Toronto Island. The sun shines everywhere except over Pete's head. He sits apart from the picnicking group, dolefully eyeing a blonde who is reading on the grass in the near distance. Feeling the resentful and hungry desperation in his glare, she picks up and moves off. Pete suggests to Joey they go for a walk, which they do after promising Betty they'll return for 'samwidges.' Pete tells Joey he wants to split Toronto and head further west, Vancouver maybe. Joey tells Pete everything's okay, he knows what his buddy needs. You guessed it: Yonge Street.

That evening, there's a brief return to the old giddiness, but even that's punctured by the waiter in the tavern who kicks the boys out of his establishment for swearing. Then the H-bomb drops. In a washroom, Joey tells Pete Bets is pregnant and he's marrying her, effectively making any break for Vancouver impossible. Pete is angry and punches a condom dispenser. He's not interested in being anybody's best man: 'You screw up your life if you want to buddy boy. Me, I'm on the move. I gotta lot of places to go and things to do and plans, see? You think I need you?'

The marriage reception is in a legion hall. It's one of the movie's most poignant and desperate scenes, and only came about because at the last minute Bradley recruited a number of street associates to act as extras on the offer of free beer.

Joey and Bets sit at the head table, their respective bouffants sadly sprinkled with confetti. Pete's up there too, and he's abject. He makes a lame speech in honour of the union, Joey follows with a slurred declaration of love and commitment in the face of what everybody already knows ('It's true we are going to have us a little family ...'). Then it's over. The final wedding scenes unfold against white walls: Joey reassuring Betty their life will be good (an exchange that ends with a lingering close-up of Bets staring into the void), Joey bumming twenty bucks from his best man to cover the booze he can't really afford but has clearly drunk his fair share of. 'Hey, ah, no hard feelings, eh?' pleads Joey. 'Beat it ya hamburger,' says his buddy.

The crash over, the movie regains its stillness and Pete crawls from the wreckage.

He walks. It's Pete's most dispirited montage, his key solo stroll through the urban ruins. The emphasis here is on the leper: Pete looks in shop windows at wedding cakes, at couples falling in the right side of love, at a whole happy city that seems to have what he can't get. The sky is as grey as that over Cape Breton, and he drinks alone.

Pete visits Joey and Bets in their new home, which is in an apartment building with a view of the skyline in the distance.[6] The furnishings are sparse but new, and Bets would offer Pete a beer but the fridge is empty and Joey isn't home yet. He can, however, stay for Kraft Dinner if he likes. When Joey enters he begins to show Pete the wonders of credit shopping: the roomful of furnishings purchased straight off the back of the *TV Guide*, the apartment intercom that dispenses muzak on tap, the colour TV. Pete warns Joey about 'getting in so deep so fast.' His buddy brushes it off. 'If the folks back home could see Joey Mayle now!' The next day, or so the cutting makes it seem, they are laid off.

Back at the new apartment, Pete and Joey are drinking beer when Bets walks in. 'What are we going to do?' she nearly sobs at the news. After all, she's going to have to leave the restaurant for the baby pretty soon. Joey, ever the addle-brained, brew-fortified optimist, tries to reassure both his wife and his buddy that everything's going to be okay. He offers Pete another beer and a place to sleep on the new hide-a-bed. Later, in the darkness, Pete hears Joey trying to calm his wife.

There won't be many words spoken for the remainder of the movie, because what is there to say? Even Joey's irrepressible optimism will imminently expire beneath the weight of what's come down, and even the feeblest attempts at conversation won't stand a chance against the crowding din of what can't be closed out: the noise of the car wash where the boys work for a day or so, the rumble, crash, and shudder of the bowling alley where Pete sets up pins alongside other men one step outside of the Sally Ann, the dismissive drone of the U.I. employee who tells the guys they haven't worked long enough to collect pogey. Of course Betty and Joey lose their apartment, and the first night that the three of them spend in their wretched east-end rooming house – which stinks of urine and has cops roaming its corridors – everyone lies awake listening to the horrible sound of a woman wailing somewhere in another room. The married couple and the best buddy are separated by a sheet.

Still, *Goin' Down the Road* finds moments of acute poetic eloquence in this desperate din, as though it has been waiting to hit this very bottom all along. If anything, the movie is at its most natural, confident and poised at precisely the intersection where all hope is abandoned, all delusion dried up, and all dreams exhausted. While snow falls with stupefying thematic appropriateness on leaves still green, the boys deliver supermarket flyers through Rosedale. On a cold day in the park at Allan Gardens, the trio join an impromptu singalong – that extraordinary moment of raw vérité beauty – which ends when a bottle smashes to the pavement and even the winos stumble off, one tossing an overcoat – in charity? contempt? frustration? – on the ground as he leaves.

In the flophouse, the silence following another hopeless conversation is filled by the Satie record Pete pulls out, and each character is captured in private reverie: Joey, Bets, and Pete all listen, the music evoking something imprecise but palpably moving to them, and to us everything that never was. But it isn't just the music that plays on our sense of things peripherally remembered. The close-ups of the faces against the walls are all echoes of earlier moments in the lives of Pete, Betty, and Joey, when each trailed the end of a sequence with a silent stare down some private road of their own.

It's Christmas, which means not only that the calendar has finally caught up with the snow we saw earlier, but that things might actually find ways of getting worse for these people who already have it so bad. Pete has a plan for stealing the ultimate Christmas feast from Loblaws, which he and Joey execute with singular obviousness in the grocery aisles. At the cash, Joey wheels the teetering cart out to the parking lot while Pete fumbles for money, but the clerk is already suspicious. When Pete offers to retrieve his money from the car, the clerk follows and a fight breaks out. Pete is pulled from the car and pummelled to the ground, and Joey runs to the rescue with a tire iron, presumably the same with which he once fixed that flat so many, many miles ago. The two speed off in a panic without the groceries, only stopping to get help for the clerk before spending the night in the convertible shivering down by the waterfront.

Back at the rooming house, what's left of the *TV Guide* furnishings are on the sidewalk.[7] There are no more doors to enter. Joey is desperate. Bets has left for her aunt's, and Joey insists they retrieve her before following through on Pete's plan to light out for the coast. 'It ain't like you're leaving her,' Pete says, gripping his collapsing friend by the collar. 'It's just til you can get something going, some money behind you. Man this is a tough town. So there are other towns. We just gotta find them. You and me. If we stick together we're bound to hit ...'

Joey either agrees or folds, but gets in the car anyway. This time, in a reversal of the opening sequence, Pete's driving and it's Joey who leans against the passenger window. They leave the city, Pete doing his best to cheer his old friend up, the highway cresting up to a flat horizon in the distance.

Is This the One?

The first thing that struck Martin Knelman about the press screening of *Goin' Down the Road* was the fact there *was* a press screening. 'Those days, you didn't see movies in Toronto before they opened,' he told me in 2011. 'You either went to New York or Los Angeles or you saw them with everybody else. In the theatre.'[1]

Because of his documentary work, Shebib was known in town, but very few people knew anything about *Goin' Down the Road* before it was screened for the press at the New Yorker Theatre in July 1969. That would quickly change.

Knelman, an entertainment reporter and critic for nearly fifty years, remembers being at that screening. So does Robert Fulford who, under the nom de plume Marshall Delaney, was the movie critic at *Saturday Night* magazine. So does Bill Fruet. In fact, it was at the press screening that Fruet had a first inkling that Don had done it. He'd made a movie people might actually *like*.

'We knew something happened at the first screening,' Fruet said. 'I happened to be sitting behind – I can't remember who it was – one of the film critics, and he was beyond himself. He was laughing and he was clapping, he just got so *involved* in this film. And I thought, "Wow. This is going to get a good review at least." But I don't think either of us had any idea it was going to take off the way it did.'[2]

Yonge Street movie theatre, ca. 1970. Courtesy of City of Toronto
Archives, Fonds 124, file 2: f0124_fl0002_id0111.

Local critical response was gushing, with not one but two Toronto newspapers – the *Star* and the *Telegram* – instantly declaring it a milestone. In the former paper, beneath a headline declaring 'Goin' Down the Road a Great Canadian Movie,' Jim Beere described it as 'the first real English-Canadian movie, not a semi-documentary, not an art film, not an embarrassing piece of double-bill fare, but a real movie.'

'And best of all, the fact that it is Canadian is almost irrelevant. It is an excellent picture by any standard.'[3]

The *Telegram*'s Clyde Gilmour was similarly moved, momentously declaring *Road* not just 'an honest and enjoyable film' but 'certainly one of the best ever made in this country.'[4]

In *Maclean's*, Canada's national newsweekly and traditionally predisposed to limning the contours of Canadian experience, Kaspars Dzeguze wrote that *Road* was 'Canadian, though not excessively so (no Mounties or Eskimos). Moreover, the story has an authenticity beyond the settings and details that make it specifically Canadian.'[5]

In Montreal, where the fruits of something like a French-language 'national cinema' had already been evident for more than decade, Dane Lanken of the *Montreal Gazette* wrote: 'Until now, there has never been a made-in-Canada movie that was good enough to make people – here and elsewhere – sit up and notice that there is real movie-making talent right here at home. The breakthrough is *Goin' Down the Road*, a low-budget saga about two down-and-out Maritimers who journey to Toronto in search of big-money jobs and the Good Life. It's a well-made movie, humorous at times, touching and poignant at others; at no time meaningless or dull.'[6]

Saturday Night's Robert Fulford, writing as Marshall Delaney, was similarly moved by what he saw as a watershed moment. He called *Road* 'the beginning ... not only of a new independent talent in feature filmmaking but perhaps also of an era in which English-speaking Canadians, like French Canadians and scores of other peoples around the world, will finally be able to make a cinema of their own.'[7] The local reviews fuelled not only the energy and excitement at the premiere, but the sense among everyone involved that the future – for themselves, for the movie, for Canadian movies in general – was almost blindingly bright.

'Oh God,' Jayne Eastwood told me when I asked her about the premiere. 'I almost got goosebumps thinking about it, the memory was so great. Watching it was just jaw-dropping. Of course I hated myself but that's me. I remember saying to Don, "It's so beautiful, I love it. Of course I was awful." He said "No, Jayne, you're actually really good." And he wasn't one to hand out compliments. And then it just exploded from there. I mean, we were famous.'

Kind of.

'I don't know about the rest of Canada but boy were we ever famous in Toronto,' Eastwood added. 'I mean people were coming up to me all the time in restaurants. I can remember Eugene Levy has this story that when the auditions were held for *Godspell* I was sitting in the Masonic Temple waiting to go on stage. Eugene and Marty Short were sitting behind me. They had just graduated from McMaster and were like just poking each other like crazy. "That's Jayne Eastwood from *Goin' Down the Road*!" They were going crazy.'

'And Gilda Radner remembered saying when we all got *Godspell* "Look! I've got Jayne! I can just touch her. I can do anything I want. I've got Jayne Eastwood from *Goin' Down the Road*! I can touch her face and I can tweak her nose!" It was like I was like really famous from that movie. It was insane.'[8]

A few years later, in his book *This Is Where We Came In*, Knelman summarized the sense of possibility, optimism, and sometimes outright excitement Shebib's movie elicited that summer of 1970: 'We began to see the glimmerings of a truly Canadian cinema,' he wrote in 1977, a year by which those glimmerings had already seemed to twinkle into oblivion.[9] A year later, Piers Handling echoed Knelman's memory of distant hope: 'Goin' Down the Road seemed to be our first step, tentative perhaps, but opening the floodgates of self-expression. For some, the promise the film held out has not been met, neither by Shebib nor by his contemporaries, although it is probably too early to tell – after all, it's only been seven years. But mired in today's faceless reality of co-productions, turning profits, and wondering what kinds of films are going to sell internationally, times look a little bleak.'[10]

As a cinephile, critic, teacher, and independent co-op founder, Robert Fothergill had already been engaged for a few years on an uphill climb. The peak was a thriving film culture in Toronto, and the slope was slippery. Sometimes it seemed like he'd never get there, and sometimes it seemed like the destination was scant inches from reach. There were very high hopes for the movie to come along that would mark the arrival. Was this it?

'Everybody was looking for the movie that would be "The One,"' Fothergill recollected in 2011. 'That would somehow be definitively Canadian, respectable in its own right. Not a film you had to kind of defend and think "Well, for a Canadian film it's not bad." That had some kind of authenticity, local character and distinctness about it, that wasn't trying to be an American film or a kind of generic, nowhere at all sort of film, which was not uncommon. And Goin' Down the Road looked like "The One."'[11]

Before returning to the flow and ebb of the English-Canadian cinematic wave that Goin' Down the Road was so quickly presumed to mark the surging crest of, it's useful to look at some of the international reviews. The fact is, if in Canada the cultural and historical circumstances of the day couldn't help but inflate the movie to the status of national cultural statement, outside the country it was greeted for what, in some respects anyway, it really was: a noteworthy movie of modest means and obvious sensitivity, a carefully observed approximation of a life sliced from a hard slab of North American concrete.

Joey and Pete: Is This the One? Courtesy of Union Pictures.

Goin' Down the Road opened in New York in October 1970. In *New York* magazine Judith Crist wrote that Shebib's movie was 'literally a brilliant film, glittering with intelligence, perception, and integrity.'[12]

Pauline Kael, of the *New Yorker*, was especially taken with the movie's approximation of life actually lived: 'There is scarcely a false touch. The Canadian Don Shebib is so good at blending actors into locations that one has to remind oneself that this is an acted film and not a documentary. Shebib has a delicate feeling for the nuances not of traditional "class" but of the class tones that come from different educations, and he uses this gift to put in social perspective the lives of two totally un-hip boys from Nova Scotia (Doug McGrath and Paul Bradley) who come to Toronto for the legendary opportunities of the big city. Perceptively acted, though the story is too familiar and the film turns out to be a somewhat hollow triumph of craft.'[13]

In the make-or-break *New York Times*, Roger Greenspun went for broke: 'Donald Shebib's *Goin' Down the Road*, which opened yesterday at the Carnegie Hall Cinema and 34th Street East Theater, has already won best Canadian picture award at the Toronto Film Festival and has received considerable praise in at least one of its pre-reviews. It is, however, a very dull movie, and because it pretends to a kind of flat realism to certify its fiction, it lacks most of the saving graces that attend ordinary bad movies and sometimes make them fun to watch.'

Ouch. A dull movie according to America's most respected newspaper, no fun to watch, and worse, patronizing: 'In spite of its earnestness, and, to a degree, because of its earnestness, the film inevitably condescends toward its characters – placing them, understanding their motives and reactions, settling their destinies with deterministic rigor. A mostly depressed view of a depressing world, it eschews the clichés of conventional fiction only to be trapped by the banalities of its own social-studies conventions. When somebody in *Goin' Down the Road* moves into an expensive apartment, you know exactly what humiliation will follow – even though the attending deities are the Angels of Economics rather than the Avenging Fates.'[14]

Nevertheless, a couple of months later, *Road* made its way to Chicago and perhaps the most glowing critical reception it met in the United States. The writer is Roger Ebert, twenty-seven years old, and for three years the movie critic at the *Sun-Times*:

Don Shebib's *Goin' Down the Road* feels at times like a film realization of Studs Terkel's 'Hard Times,' until you remind yourself that the movie is fiction and the time is now. It tells the story of two young men from Canada's Maritime Provinces who come to the big city, Toronto, lured by the possibility of good jobs and good times. They find none of the former and precious few of the latter – a few beery, brawling evenings and a few easy girls aside – but they're game and they keep pushing until the urban monster grinds them down.

The film's special accomplishment is its treatment of the characters and the city itself with an absolutely unsentimental level-headedness. It tells a story that contains joy, silliness, love and despair. But these things are kept organic to the story; the film itself doesn't pretend to be other than a record. Shebib achieves a documentary objectivity that touches us more deeply than tear jerking could.

I don't know if I've put that clearly enough. What I mean is that *Goin' Down the Road* doesn't pander.

In the precise obverse of Greenspun's response, Ebert marvelled at the movie's many moments of utterly convincing lo-fi naturalism:

Shebib, directing Bradley and McGrath, makes these scenes so poignant and so accurate that they could represent, if necessary, the human condition. The easy male camaraderie of the two friends is so unforced that it betrays similar scenes in (John Cassavetes') *Husbands* for what they are:

three professional actors narcissistically killing time. In *Goin' Down the Road* Shebib does what the Cassavetes of *Shadows* knew how to do, and he does it better.

There are other scenes, of jobs in car washes and bowling alleys, of meeting a couple of waitresses, of Bradley getting married and moving into an apartment and buying three rooms of furniture on time payments. Then winter comes. They're laid off at the bottling plant, and that would seem too obvious in a more contrived film, but in this film it's just simply what happens. *Goin' Down the Road* is about hard times here and now, and it's the best movie to hit town in a long time.[15]

Ebert's glowing review ran a month or so after Shebib's movie was screened at the London Film Festival. There it was seen by Dilys Powell, who had been reviewing movies at the *Sunday Times* since 1939, the year after Don Shebib was born. She saw the movie shortly after seeing Greek director Theo Angelopoulous's *The Reconstruction*, and found it (more or less) measured up. Her comments are contained in a list-like survey of 'foreign' films at the festival: 'And a Canadian film, *Goin' Down the Road*. This is astonishingly accomplished, more accomplished than the Greek piece, though personally I miss the pleasure of recognition. Two young men set off by car for Toronto. They leave passable jobs in Nova Scotia for the dream of better jobs, easy money, the rich life; one sees them momentarily successful, then sliding into unemployment, squalor, crime. The playing, subtle beneath its aggressive surface, of Doug McGrath and Paul Bradley brilliantly conveys the fecklessness, the drifting stupidity of the pair; and we are surely going to hear more of the director Don Shebib.'[16]

Missing 'the pleasure of recognition' is a revealing phrase, especially when compared to the excitement of seeing something like home experienced by so many Canadian critics. As for those 'passable jobs in Nova Scotia' Powell claims Pete and Joey leave behind, one can only wonder at what she saw, and whether it was a scene from this or another movie at the festival. The point is, Powell – like a number of non-Canadian critics – saw the movie unburdened by national cultural expectations, and the movie she saw was significantly different from the one seen back home.

In his 1978 book *The Films of Don Shebib*, Piers Handling wrote about a certain attraction exerted by *Goin' Down the Road*, an attraction – at least in part – apparently shared by many of the people who passed through the doors of the New Yorker in those opening weeks: 'I still vividly remember the first time I saw *Goin' Down the Road*. It was sometime in the fall of 1970. I was living in Kingston, and in my last year of university, studying in a field unrelated to film. But we had all heard of it – its reputation had travelled quickly. And there it was: a truly entertaining film full of gutsy energy and a raw power that impressed through its grimy veracity. But I don't remember it for that. It was more because for the first time, here was a reflection of something that lay just around the corner – the Yonge Street strip at night, Sam the Record Man open until all hours, Toronto Island, and those gaudy and rudimentary taverns where they were all drinking Canadian beer – Molson's, Labatt's! This is what we all reacted to in a large part, something immediately identifiable, a type of visual short-hand and we all filled in the gaps because we knew it all so well. This was what it was like – that was what we were like. It wasn't New York, Paris or London; it was unmistakably Toronto, and many of us had been to Sam's, we'd shopped in that same store. Not only that, but I saw the film in a theatre where I had also seen the Paul Newmans, the Julie Christies and the Dustin Hoffmans on the same screens.'[17]

That Handling's book begins with this – a recollection of the movie's sheer power of place – certainly reveals something of its impact on Toronto audiences in those first weeks and months of release. No small part of the film's connection with contemporary local audiences had as much to do with the local nature of its setting as the socio-economic nature of its message. That that came second, if at all, is evident in Handling's 'that was what we were like.' An Upper Canadian graduate of European boarding schools and a Queen's University student of history and philosophy, Handling was in fact not 'like' Pete or Joey at all. But what he shared was the place in which their story transpired and, at the time anyway, that was sufficient to convey a powerful sense of connection to Shebib's hardscrabble on-the-outs world.

'Even though it was working-class guys, I think it was still a film that so many of us could relate to,' Handling stressed over forty years later. 'Even though we were quote middle-class well-to-do students going to a place like Queen's, one of the establishment universities in the country, there was just such recognition with those guys.'[18]

When Handling saw the movie, it was in a commercial cinema in Kingston, Ontario. He was nineteen years old, had returned to Canada after spending five years at a British boarding school in Germany, and didn't really know Toronto all that well apart from the experience he'd had appearing as an actor in a film shot there by another Queen's student. That was enough.

'I knew Toronto through working on that short film,' he told me in 2011. 'The Yonge Street strip was so famous. The record stores, A&A's and Sam's: we went to those record stores whenever we came to Toronto. The Island, et cetera. Just seeing those parts of the city on film in a real regular commercial cinema, and not in the Queen's film department on a small, postage-stamp-sized screen. It was probably the first Canadian film I had seen in that way.'

'And of course the spirit of the film was something,' he added. 'The beer drinking, the guys, the irresponsibility, looking for jobs in the big city. I was about a year away from graduation, so you were thinking a little bit about some of the same concerns these guys had. Getting involved in relationships, unwanted pregnancies.'

'Not that that happened to me,' Handling clarified. 'But it was certainly in the air at that time.'[19]

It would seem that the sheer fact of the movie's unmistakable *Canadianness*, let alone its unabashed casting of Toronto as Toronto, played no small part in its initial embrace by movie-goers, especially so in Toronto. Never mind that the New Yorker on Yonge was the kind of arty movie house that guys like Pete and Joey would never patronize, and never mind that the movie's view of Toronto is that of an alienated outsider confronted by a concrete fortress of unwelcoming indifference, this was something like home.

Among the contexts in which *Goin' Down the Road*'s eventual status as cultural milestone must be considered is its inescapable documentation of Toronto, a city hitherto almost weirdly invisible in feature films. Indeed, apart from little-seen 1960s films like Don Owen's *Nobody Waved Good-bye* or David Sector's *Winter Kept Us Warm* and *The Offering*, Toronto on film largely meant Toronto on TV. You'd see it in news reports, car lot commercials, and the occasional TV show like *Wojeck*, but never in a movie theatre. In this respect, at least initially, *Goin' Down the Road* was groundbreaking.

Robert Fothergill was deeply immersed in the project of trying to promote a local film culture in Toronto at the time *Road* appeared. Along with people like David Cronenberg, Lorne Lipowitz (who would later become *Saturday Night Live* creator Lorne Michaels), and John Hofsess, he was one of the founders of the Canadian Filmmakers Distribution Centre, a collective devoted to the promotion, distribution, and screening of made-in-Canada movies. Like many of his contemporaries, the English-born Fothergill was steeped in movie culture: the European art-house scene, the campus film-club circuit, avant-garde and low-budget screening events, anything that might help fuel the idea that Toronto was not only interested in movies, it *made* movies.

Those were the days, Fothergill told me in 2011, when everything

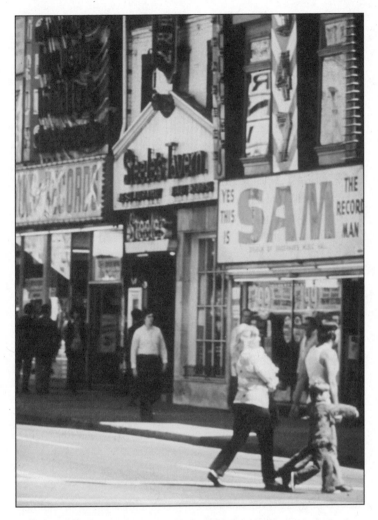

Yonge and Dundas, ca. 1970: 'Something like here.' Courtesy of
City of Toronto Archives, Fonds 200, series 1465, file 312: s1465_
fl03123_it0051.

exciting that happened seemed to be happening somewhere else, especially cinematically. As much as local people like himself worked to build an enthusiastic audience for underground, experimental, and other forms of off-Hollywood motion picture spectacle in Toronto, one still seemed to have to look at places like London, Paris, New York, and even (for God's sake) Montreal to see how it was really done. Toronto just seemed utterly uninterested in seeing itself as a movie town. As a place to see Hollywood movies maybe, but as a place where interesting movies got made? And where an audience interested in them gathered and watched? That was somewhere else. This felt something like *here*.

'What was striking was the Canadian-ness,' Fothergill observed in 2011, 'or more particularly the Toronto-ness, because Vancouver films and Montreal films were quite different. It was kind of lower class, Parkdale-area, gritty streets, taverns, manufacturing areas, marginalized people. And that seemed somehow more authentic for Toronto than attempts to do a more glossy, bourgeois, running-along-Yorkville kind of thing.'

'And it already seemed in a kind of time warp,' he added, 'because what it represented was a Toronto which in some ways had been perhaps more like the 1950s than 1969. Toronto was already a pretty – as they would say then – swinging kind of a place. We'd had Expo, and we'd had the Centennial. And all kinds of things were happening. And yet the film that seemed to say "This is Toronto. We know where this is. We do live here," was a film about ne'er do well types on the fringes, not going to make it.'

Shebib had captured Toronto all right, but not the city anyone had expected to see. Where was the glamour? The money? The happening look-at-me up-and-coming northern metropolis? This place was down, dirty, cold, and indifferent, a place where hopes and dreams get off the bus and die.

Fothergill added: 'There's that scene at the end where nothing is said but a cop is coming down the stairs of the seedy rooming house that they're in. These people are not gaining anything from the upwardly mobile, trendy, Toronto. I mean there was so much money around in the late '60s. They built Ontario Place and the Ontario Science Centre and were putting up universities on every street corner, and everybody could get money in the summer to do it. It was a really thriving place in which lots of people could make it very easily. And yet here is *the* Toronto film and it's about people who aren't going to.'

'Then the fact of its sort of documentary realist kind of style, but that too seemed to be indigenously Canadian. The Richard Leiterman handheld camera, the grab-what-you-can actuality sound, real locations, real lighting. All that kind of thing. And though it may not make for a particularly attractive film, it says this is the real place. We know this, somehow.'[20]

Here, after all, was a movie that not only displayed Toronto, it displayed a side of the city that contradicted the usual upbeat image of the town as a thriving, upscale, hip, urban travel destination. Yorkville seemed a long way from the Yonge Street strip where Pete and Joey prowled for girls and down-home companionship, where the freshly erected towers of the new City Hall and Toronto-Dominion buildings cast nothing but shadows. This was a city of the struggling, the displaced, and the marginal, a site of socio-economic inequity, a place less defined by projected desire than hard-fought struggle. It may have been the Toronto lived in by thousands of residents, but it certainly wasn't the city anyone had made a movie about. In this sense, the feeling of epiphany was startling. For many viewers, Fothergill among them, *Goin' Down the Road* captured the city they lived in. It felt not just like the first English Canadian movie that seemed to matter, it felt like the first Toronto movie ever made.

It wasn't, of course – *A Dangerous Age*, *Nobody Waved Good-bye*, *Winter Kept Us Warm*, and *The Offering* had come before – but that it seemed so says something about the climate into which it was released. (The fact that it *had* an actual commercial release also provided it with an added aura of breakthrough.) There were certain sectors of the city's cultural imagination that needed *Goin' Down the Road*, that saw in it the arrival of something long overdue.

To understand this point, and to fully comprehend the tone of exhilarated gratitude in some of those first reviews, one must also consider the surging sense of cultural nationalism in English Canada at the time. It was the late 1960s. Pierre Trudeau, the charismatic, starlet-dating pop star prime minister, was in office, which is where John and Yoko came to visit him in 1969. Expo '67 had drawn the approving attention of the world a couple of years earlier, but that – as per Trudeau – was a mixed blessing: it had taken place in Montreal, and one of the key sources of Anglo-Canadian cultural envy at the time was Quebec's feisty emergent nationalism. At the time when defiant French Canadian culture was thriving – politically, musically, literarily, and cinematically – English Canada seemed stalled. Already, signs of the great defection were everywhere: Neil Young had headed for the States, as had fellow musicians Robbie Robertson and The Band, David Clayton-Thomas, and Joni Mitchell. Canada's best-known filmmaker, Toronto's Norman Jewison, was a made guy in Hollywood, and Canada's most famous actors – Christopher Plummer, William Shatner, Susan Clark, John Vernon, Michael Sarrazin – were far more likely to be called that by Canadians than in the America where they now lived and worked. This was the vacuum that *Goin' Down the Road* seemed not only to fill but defy: it had parked here and would not budge.

One of the early beneficiaries of cultural subsidy largesse, in the form of the $19,000 prize from the recently established Canadian Film Development Corporation, *Goin' Down the Road* also seemed to confirm the legitimacy of organized and legislated efforts to promote English Canadian culture. It is in no way coincidental that the timing of its re-

lease also coincided with the first flowerings of Canadian theatre, literature, and Canadian content regulations on radio. (It was also, one feels
compelled to note, released a year after an organized demonstration on
Parliament Hill in Ottawa to protest the cancellation of the much-be-
loved Maritime hoedown show *Don Messer's Jubilee*.) There was a definite
sense of concentrated cultural assertiveness in the air, that an English
Canadian culture was not only worth having but rallying round the flag
for, and in this sense at least, Pete and Joey were, if not heroes, at least
symbols of the legitimacy of the struggle.

'This was post Expo '67,' Piers Handling reminds me in 2011. 'There
was this increasing pride in Canada as a country, a strong sense we were
colonized by America and the UK, and there was a growing and emerging nationalism that we kind of all felt.'

'It was also the beginning of an artistic renaissance after what I think
was probably a long sleep,' Handling recalls. 'Leonard Cohen, Gordon
Lightfoot, that was all going on. As I said I'd been out of the country for
five years, so *Goin' Down the Road* was really my first connection to my
own culture after having been away. And it was this awareness that the
cinematic landscape, that my cinema adventures, could actually con-
tain a Canadian film – and perhaps other Canadian films – that was a
complete revelation to me. It was very, very exciting.'[21]

Peter Harcourt was teaching in the film department at Queen's at
the time Handling was a student. But he hadn't seen *Goin' Down the Road*
when it first came out. After studying at Cambridge and working at
the British Film Institute in London, where he first started writing and
thinking about Canadian films as an emergent but tentative national
cinema, he had been back in Canada for a few years. At Queen's Harcourt deepened his intellectual investigation of Canadian movies, and
Shebib's first film seemed exemplary of something Harcourt was only
beginning to formulate.

'I really wasn't there for *Goin' Down the Road*,' he told me in 2011. 'I

Toronto City Hall, ca. 1970: The shining city, sort of. Courtesy of City of Toronto Archives, Fonds 124, file 2: f0124_fl0002_id0003.

sort of inherited the film from people that went before me. As for its iconic status, I probably played a part in that, as did Piers and as did Rob Fothergill. But to speak for myself, I liked these "little" films. I thought that's what Canadian film should be.'

'So I liked the modest dimensions of the film,' he added, 'the budget of the film, and I would celebrate those as being as exemplary for Canadian film at that time. But that was my ideology of "little" Canadian films because I came into Canadian film when it was still basically a cottage industry. My championing of Jean Pierre Lefebvre was very much a part of that, as well. It was a cottage industry, films made for no money at all, made as if for one's own personal friends, which hopefully would be as sufficiently large as the cost of production if the cost of production was modest enough. And Godard was talking like that in those days. He was saying "You can make film for one hundred thousand dollars as long as you can get one hundred thousand people to pay one dollar to see it."'

'That kind of stuff. It was very different, there wasn't an industrial model. A very different production model than what we have today. Because there was not yet a television industry as there is today. So that was sort of my own, to a certain extent, appropriation of the film.'[22]

Harcourt's first writing on Shebib's films didn't appear until 1976, in *Cinema Canada*. By that time, Shebib's first film had become well established as a landmark – albeit a 'little' one – but it was Harcourt who was instrumental in accounting for precisely why that land was worth marking. It wasn't because the movie had facilitated any 'breakthrough' in English Canadian movies, nor was it because it had markedly changed the way most people thought about Canadian movies, if they thought about them at all. It was because there was something distinctive in its hesitant but unblinking vision of people simply struggling to function in a world that seemed beyond them, in its frank admission of how difficult just getting on could be. For Harcourt, this was the big revelation in this 'little' movie. And exactly where it marked the abyss between itself and Hollywood.

Given the blustery atmospheric activity, the wide range of critical response, and how disparately his movie was read, misread, interpreted, misinterpreted, praised, and damned, perhaps Shebib's antipathy towards critics is at least partly understandable. Partly. On the subject of movie criticism, Shebib had this to say to John Hofsess in 1975: 'It's all politics,' he said, 'and ego-tripping. I'm not going into the matter of who *writes* well. I'm talking about what motivates them, and how a film gets treated. It's corrupt.'

'What I'm saying,' he added by way of clarification, 'is that if I preview a film for Judith Crist, say, and she likes it, I can pretty well be assured that *that* fact alone will ensure that two or three other critics will attack my film; they will *use* my film to attack her. That's what I call the critic's bullshit game.'[23]

Victims of the Rainbow

In 1972, after *Goin' Down the Road* had made Shebib's name but did nothing to pre-empt the commercial failure of his follow-up movie *Rip-Off* (a bleakly comic exercise in countercultural revisionism about suburban kids who fail dismally at starting a commune in northern Ontario), a book appeared that would prove instrumental in re-framing Shebib's assertive expression of distinctive national identity as a drag on emergent English-Canadian self-actualization. Within just a couple of years of being hailed as the beginning of a new era in the cinematic representation of the Anglo-Canuck experience, *Road* was being condemned as a dead end.

The book was *Survival*, poet and novelist Margaret Atwood's eminently debatable thematic analysis of Canadian literature. In it, Atwood took Northrop Frye's concept of the 'garrison mentality' in Canadian fiction to the next level. She saw the tendency in the English Canadian literary imagination towards stories of victimized solipsism as an indication of a shared consciousness of colonial retardation, a coast-to-coast pathology of agoraphobic despair. For Canadians, she suggested, the primary struggle was not expression or identity, but just getting by. Indeed, getting by *was* the Canadian experience and identity. If the defining American mythic experience was transcendent individual achievement, Canadians were just trying to trudge from one disappointment to the next.

'Certainly Canadian authors spend a disproportionate amount of time making sure that their heroes die or fail,' she wrote in the book's introduction. 'Much Canadian writing suggests that failure is required because it is felt – consciously or unconsciously – to be the only "right" ending, the only thing that will support the characters' (or their authors') view of the universe. When such endings are well handled and consistent with the whole book, one can't quarrel with them on aesthetic grounds. But when Canadian writers are writing clumsy or manipulated endings, they are much less likely to manipulate in a positive than they are in a negative direction: that is, the author is less likely to produce a sudden inheritance from a rich old uncle or the surprising news that his hero is really the son of a Count than he is to conjure up an unexpected natural disaster or an out-of-control car, tree or minor character so that the protagonist may achieve a satisfactory failure. Why should this be so? Could it be that Canadians have a will to lose which is as strong and pervasive as the Americans' will to win?'[1]

Atwood's primary object was literary. But the condition she describes – this 'will to lose' which the quote above ascribes not to Canadian literature but 'Canadians' – is too insidiously entrenched in the national psyche to be contained on the page. Apparently, it's hardwired into the fact of Canadian-ness. Elsewhere she adds: 'Just to round things out, we might add that the two English Canadian feature films (apart from Allan King's documentaries) to have had much success so far, *Goin' Down The Road* and *The Rowdyman*, are both dramatizations of failure. The heroes survive, but just barely; they are born losers, and their failure to do anything but keep alive has nothing to do with the Maritime Provinces or "regionalism." It's pure Canadian, from sea to sea.'[2]

Coming as it did in the aftermath of the great surge in Canadian nationalist thinking – which saw the legislated creation of several programs, like the Canadian Film Development Corporation, which granted Shebib the start-up funds to make *Road*, to encourage the production and development of 'distinctly Canadian' culture – *Survival* marked a sudden and deafening screeching of brakes on the highway to a Canadian cultural identity. It argued that we already had an identity, but that what we were was nothing to be proud of. *Born* losers.

Within a couple of years of its appearance, *Survival* was bearing heavily on the project of Canadian film criticism, itself a mere stripling sprung from the freshly turned soil of the nationalist impulse. And Pete and Joey, as the most conspicuous embodiments of English Canadian cinematic fiction, suddenly became freighted by even more external baggage. Formerly standard-bearers for the possibility of what we could become – people punishingly yet proudly inhabiting an unmistakably Canadian fictional realm – they were symbols of what we didn't want to be.

In a 1973 *Take One* essay that became something of a *Survival* for Canadian cinema studies, Robert Fothergill outlined the archetypes of bornloserdom in English fiction film. Although he cited a number of movies made before and since *Road*, the film loomed over 'Coward, Bully, or Clown: The Dream-Life of a Younger Brother'[3] like a great, grey, sodden cloud. His subject was the male figure in Canadian movies, a figure which, in Fothergill's conception (and one most certainly apt when applied to the mythic imperative of Hollywood), stood for national identity itself.

In 2011, Fothergill tried to contextualize the thinking that had motivated the article. Quite simply, there seemed to be an awful lot of sorry guys stumbling darkly through Canadian movies. 'On the basis of a fairly small selection,' he told me, '[the essay] seemed to be diagnosing something peculiar. A peculiar sort of malaise of the imagination that came out in these films. It did not say that all Canadians at the time were cowards, bullies or clowns, but that it seemed difficult to imagine movie protagonists who were courageous, resourceful, effective, articulate, et cetera. They just didn't look real on the Canadian screen somehow.'[4]

As he wrote: 'What, then, is the version of *le condition canadienne* reflected to us by our feature films? It is the depiction, through many different scenarios, of the radical inadequacy of the male protagonist – his moral failure, especially, and most visibly, in his relationships with women. One film after another is like a recurring dream which takes its space from the dreamer's guilty consciousness of his own essential impotence.'[5]

Although Fothergill now looks back at some of the methodology and conclusions reached in the essay as 'naive,' he still maintains there was something conspicuously persistent in this apparent dramatic fascination Canadian movies had with 'radically inadequate' male figures. He was just trying to figure out why. The essay 'was trying to see something in the movies that was common to quite a lot of them and did seem to be there,' he explained. 'The question is what you make of that. Do you see it as a symptom of something? And is it a symptom of something to be kind of worried and dismayed about? First thing, does it actually represent some element of the collective psychic state of Canadians? Well hardly, surely. Does it represent only something about people trying to create movies or create art? Or more generally perhaps in Canada that there was a slightly doomed sense of inadequacy and failure? I don't quite get that either. I mean Don Shebib himself isn't some sort of klutzy loser guy. Of the three categories he's more of the bully than the coward or the clown, I think.'[6]

Yet if one elevates the phallic destinies of Canadian-made movie protagonists to the level of cultural imperative, Pete and Joey are doomed to an especially conspicuous flaccidity. Arriving in Toronto with dreams of erotic conquest ('Hide your daughters!'), their disappointment in matters sexual is as unrelentingly systematic – and therefore arguably emblematic – as their failure to achieve wealth, sustained employment, and even happiness. This is what qualifies them so boldly as avatars of Fothergill's archetypal triptych of Canadian male fuck-ups.

As he wrote: 'On another socio-economic level (from the equally under-actualized middle-class male losers in Clarke Mackey's *The Only Thing You Know* and George Kaczender's *Don't Let the Angels Fall*), Joey, played by Paul Bradley in Don Shebib's *Goin' Down the Road*, has a good deal of the Coward about him. Bewildered by big-city life, and with a tendency to get maudlin drunk, he finally runs out of the whole mess, leaving a pregnant and newly-evicted wife to fend for herself.'

'When times are good, Joey and his friend Peter (Doug McGrath) caper about with childish irresponsibility, drinking and frolicking in a fashion that is likeable enough but rather trying to the women who have to put up with it. Peter's repertoire includes a humiliatingly un-successful attempt to ingratiate himself with a sexy French lady, Nicole Morin. In their antics, the Canadian male as Coward can be seen shad-ing into another incarnation: the Clown.'[7]

As a menu of archetypes, none of Fothergill's types were especially appetizing, and all seemed to signify a certain fundamental failure of follow-through in the Canadian male cinematic character, what Fother-gill elsewhere in the essay described as a 'deep-down gutlessness.' While one could (and some subsequently would) take issue with Fothergill's equation of dramatic failure with a national condition; his readings of certain Canadian movies in such deterministically phallocentric terms; or gender politics which elevate even male failure to the primary spec-tacle on hand, 'Coward, Bully, or Clown: The Dream-Life of a Younger Brother' had inestimable impact. Peter Harcourt, an early film depart-ment appointee at York University and founder of the film studies pro-gram at Queen's, would become a key figure in the academic study of and serious critical inquiry into Canadian movies as a national cinema. Harcourt has said it was Fothergill's essay that first put a frame around something that had otherwise seemed so formless as to barely exist. Harcourt, without whom the serious academic study of Canadian film is near unimaginable, credits Fothergill with making thinking about Canadian movies in thematic terms possible.

A year after the article appeared, Harcourt opened the books on the academic scrutiny of Canadian film. 'I first introduced Canadian film at York in 1974,' he said in 2011, 'as a section in a course on foreign cinema. So I showed four weeks of Italian Neorealism, four weeks of Canadian film – I showed them *Goin' Down the Road* – and then four weeks of Japanese. And so I had students do these wonderful essays comparing Pete and Joey's quest and Genjuro in *Ugetsu Monogatari*. Not good film criticism, but good stuff for a first year course. And I sent the one essay off to Shebib comparing Genjuro and Pete and Joey because he has such a low opinion of the academic study of film. But that was the space I was in. Sort of Gatling gun approach, all over the place, because I wasn't really focused on anything, but bit by bit the Canadian thing got into my pores.'

According to Harcourt, it was Fothergill's essay that helped in that regard: it was the piece that opened those pores. 'Robert's "Coward, Bully, or Clown" did for film what Atwood's book on *Survival* did for literature,' he said. 'It was a road map and it really affected my way of dealing with these films because once you have something like that written, you can show films that exemplify it. Which is dangerous if you don't show other films but very valuable if you're a teacher.'[8]

Fothergill, incidentally, disagrees with this, although he finds it flattering. He insists that Harcourt was the trail-blazer, with his writings on things like the National Film Board's Unit B, Don Owen's *Nobody Waved Good-Bye*, and Gilles Groulx's *Le Chat dans le sac*, all of which appeared several years before 'Coward, Bully, or Clown.'

For his part, Harcourt stresses that the salient point about Fothergill's essay wasn't that it introduced him to Canadian film, but that it provided him with a framework in which to think about it, and it was within that framework that *Goin' Down the Road* began to loom as something significant: the magnetic pole around which certain hitherto scattered thoughts on a national cinema gathered and began to take shape. If Fothergill had provided a structure in which to think in thematic terms about English Canadian movies, *Goin' Down the Road* emerged as the model in which Harcourt's previous explorations of a possible national cinema began to cohere into something like a pattern. Perhaps even an identity.

'Having explored these extraordinary documentaries at the Film Board,' he told me in 2011, 'and been excited by them, and having met Rob, knowing his position and knowing that article, and finally seeing *Goin' Down the Road*, I felt, in my weaning away from my addiction to European cinema – which I was still at in 1970 – that there was something in these Canadian films that would constitute a cinema, something that I could talk about, that *could* be talked about. There could be a discourse.'

'That was very important for me personally,' he explained, 'and perhaps for the cinema itself that there was a body of work to be talked about. While I was still at Queen's, I sort of illegally set up a cinematheque in the evenings, and I found I could get all these Quebec films, so I brought them in. I'd never heard of these films but I showed them the first Jean Pierre Lefebvre films and I showed *Le chat dans le sac* and I thought, "Hello, hello, hello. There's something going on here." So I wrote that piece on *Le chat dans le sac* and *Nobody Waved Good-bye* to say that. That there *is* a cinema to be discussed. That was the exciting thing for me.'

'Then Shebib's film confirmed my sense, along with the stuff I had seen from Quebec that there was some really good stuff going on.'[9]

It might have been a little Canadian movie, but it wasn't size that mattered. In its very modesty, it carried something 'we' – as English

Canadians seeking a sort of cultural affirmation – could call our very own.

Yet that thinking could sometimes be burdensome, especially for the weight it pressed upon little movies like *Goin' Down the Road* and 'poor souls' like Pete and Joey. For all Shebib, Fruet, Leiterman, Mc-Grath, and Bradley's attempts to keep these two westward drifters as naturalistic, unembellished, and bone-simple as possible, by the mid-1970s they were symbols: representatives not only of the national imagination but of its self-defeating, self-colonizing, and self-sabotaging inner child – the younger brother doomed forever to a state of terminally envious, paralysing insecurity.

As far back as 1970, Robert Fulford's *Saturday Night* piece on the film had been titled 'Two Losers, Lost in Toronto.' By 1975, when *MacLean's* critic John Hofsess sat down to interview Shebib for his book *Inner Views: Ten Canadian Film-Makers*, the writer had had enough. Indeed, he seemed so moved to indignation by terminal masculine ineffectuality in Canadian cinema that he took it up with a key perpetrator: Don Shebib.

In his introduction, Hofsess wrote: 'In the future when people talk about Canadian movies, and really mean *Canadian* movies, these are the film directors (who included not only Shebib but Claude Jutra, Denys Arcand, William Fruet, Jack Darcus and even Pierre Berton), and these are the influential films, that are bound to be discussed. For these are the dreamers of independent mind and unique vision who said "No" to American mass culture; thus a new culture began to germinate.'[10]

Nevertheless, the 'No' articulated by Shebib, which might well be expressed in *Goin' Down the Road*'s very denial of the conventionally triumphant Hollywood male, was not a satisfactory 'No.' It was 'Not enough.'

As Hofsess wrote: 'Think of *Goin' Down the Road*, *Wedding in White*, *Mon Oncle Antoine*, *The Rowdyman*, *Paperback Hero*: good stories, fine acting, profoundly poignant moments, but nowhere a character with the brains, balls, will or gall to master life as it must be lived in the twentieth century. Instead we have a continuing stream of characters who cope, barely and mope, plenty.'[11]

Citing Atwood, Hofsess proceeded to hold Shebib to account for his persistent depiction of Canadians as 'losers,' apparently evident not just in *Goin' Down the Road* but also in *Rip-Off* and *Between Friends*, neither of which had exactly caught fire at the box office. Hofsess appeared to know why. 'There is another common characteristic in Canadian films,' he told Shebib, 'and more to the point *your* films, and that is that the city is always cast in a hostile light; technology is a terrible thing, urban life is dehumanizing. So many of our films take place in *small* towns, or out in the country somewhere, it again suggests that we are shrinking from a sophisticated mastery of the complex world we live in. In real life, Canadians are busy building computer centres, nuclear reactors, engaging in advanced medical research, and the like; but, so far, our movies do not reflect that activity, and do not reflect the many and considerable successes of Canadians in those fields.'

'Instead,' he went on, 'over and over, we take this view of life, from the bottom. I'm suggesting to you that one of the important reasons that *Between Friends* failed commercially is that it did not give audiences any fulfilment of their aspirations. The mood of Canadian film-goers is changing, and you were caught, off guard, by the change. They didn't want another story about emotional and intellectual cripples, no matter how well done it was.'[12]

Not surprisingly, the man charged with the crippling of his characters, and being out of step with the changing Canadian cultural mood, wasn't having any of it. 'Maybe. I don't know,' Shebib replied. 'Though actually I think the film was misrepresented and over-simplified in the press. People read about it, and based on what they read, they said, "Oh we don't want to see that." *Failures, losers,* I hate words like that. I see the film as being about some average but interesting people who *happen* to fail, which isn't the same thing as saying it's about failure.'

Hofsess persisted. 'Can you agree that Canadian films – to which you have contributed three features now, and a number of shorts – seem to have a tragic sense of life?' Shebib, whom Hofsess had previously (and, especially in the context of this exchange, unsurprisingly) characterized as having hated Atwood's *Survival* 'on the grounds that it is bullshit' and harbouring 'a dislike for analysis of his movies,' replied: 'I don't see the sense of making that a Canadian characteristic, that's all.'[13]

Looking back in 2011 on the debate he was instrumental in generating back in 1973, Robert Fothergill remained somewhat surprised by the sheer mileage his 'little piece' had enjoyed. But only somewhat. When describing the climate of defensive cultural boosterism of the era in which *Road* was released, when people like Fothergill and his Canadian Filmmakers Distribution cohorts were actively engaged in the promotion of an English Canadian film culture in a Toronto that didn't seem to care much, he describes a time when it seemed reasonable not only to insist that English Canada have a culture, but also to suggest what kind of culture that might be.

Nearly forty years after its publication, I asked Fothergill to what extent he still stood behind the theory his essay espoused. 'There's very little theory behind it,' he laughed. 'I remember my colleague Peter Morris taking the article apart once because it assumes a fairly unproblematic reflection of reality, that films show us what life is like, and we know it's not quite that simple. And yet, and *yet* ...'

'So I'm not sure that it really proved anything or made a particularly sensible case. What's interesting is that over the decades now, every now and then somebody would review a new Canadian movie and cite my little article and say "Look! It's still happening!" Or would phone me up and we'd have a little chat about it.'[14]

Nevertheless, he says, there *was* something decidedly conspicuous going on as regards the depiction of men in the English Canadian movies of the day. And, while the sample might have been rather small for the purposes of broader cultural conclusions, and while it might have been, as he now says, 'naive' to make such a simple and direct connection between the dramatic content of a few movies and the ideological proclivities of their culture at large, he does remain struck at just how tenacious those cowards, bullies, and clowns at the time were. And how they'd pop up in the darndest places.

'In my own first play, called *Detaining Mr. Trotsky*,' Fothergill told me, 'which I started writing as early as about 1977, but which didn't come out until '87, the protagonist is a younger brother figure with a very troubled, conflicted identity, torn between loyalty to the British parent, in the form of the British colonel who tells him what to do, but also drawn toward the rebellious foreigner revolutionary Trotsky, and who exhibits considerable cowardice in trying to pass off the blame for revealing Trotsky's location to the Jewish translator, and who will go off to France and be killed in three weeks.'

The coward, the bully, and the clown, all present and accounted for in a single character, and a character created by Robert Fothergill, born in Britain but apparently very deeply entrenched in Canada. 'It took someone else to point this out to me,' he told me in 2011, 'and when they did, I thought "My god, I've done exactly the same thing." Now either that means I've fully bought into the Canadian psyche or that all I was writing about in the first place was myself. Which is possible.'[15]

Reminded of all this chatter in 2011, Shebib shook his head. Sensitivity lingered. 'If you base anything on any kind of statistical analysis, an example of two or three is hardly a statistical analysis,' he said. 'Yes those two films (*Road* and *Between Friends*) are about losers if you want to use that word. I object to that word. A loser is someone who rolls over and dies. Pete and Joey were fighters. They might have lost but they're not losers, and in this film [that is, the 2011 sequel] Pete wins.'

'So to not only brand a whole culture but to brand any particular filmmaker as someone who has only made films about losers ...,' he trailed off, took a deep breath, and cleared his throat.

'I mean I believe, *completely believe*, that this is a very sick country. It has really deep psychological problems. Of accepting its own success. You know the old expression in Hollywood that you're only as good as your last picture? Well that's not true, never was true. In Hollywood, ... to this day, you're only as good as your fifth last picture. If you made a good picture five pictures ago and you haven't made a good once since, *now* you're out of luck.'

'In Canada, you're not even as good as your last picture. This is a very hard country to succeed in because it's very hard for Canadians to accept success. And then when they do accept success, they make mediocrity. I don't know who said this but it's certainly true, Canada is a country where the milk rises to the top. That's what it is.'[16]

Re-surfacing

By the mid-1970s, *Goin' Down the Road* was a contentious Canadian classic and Shebib a filmmaker with a lengthening trail of commercial failures – *Rip-Off*, *Between Friends* (easily his most critically applauded film), *Second Wind*. The concept of a popular and distinctive English Canadian cinema remained a stubbornly unrealized dream, and the tiny garden plot of Canadian cinema studies was getting thick with references to movies practically no one had had an opportunity to see. (Just to test this, Robert Fothergill included an entirely fabricated movie title in his 'Coward, Bully, or Clown' essay, where it remains to this day. No one noticed and he has never been called on it.) It was the cinema that Peter Harcourt came to call 'invisible,' and yet what one saw if one could see it was a legacy of work bearing the unmistakable traces of Don Shebib's work-boot prints.

Indeed, the main reason it was possible for thinkers like Atwood and Fothergill to express alarm at the persistence of 'radical male inadequacy' in English Canadian movies was because, in its wake, *Goin' Down the Road* had seemingly fostered the making of a striking number of movies that fit the downbeat bill: not only Shebib's own follow-up films, but Fruet's *Wedding in White* (based on the writer-director's play, and featuring McGrath and Bradley as a pair of drunken war vets whose abject shenanigans leave the movie's main character pregnant, abandoned, and utterly hopeless), Peter Carter's *The Rowdyman*, Paul Lynch's supremely aptly titled *The Hard Part Begins*, Clarke Mackey's *The Only Thing You Know*, Jack Darcus's *Proxyhawks* and *Great Coups of History*, Frank Vitale's *Montreal Main*, and Peter Pearson's *Paperback Hero*.

There was, in fact, no escaping it: if you were looking to these movies as representations of a culture's attempt to express itself, and if you were compelled to interpret that expression according to the dramatic trajectory taken by the film's protagonists, English Canada was undergoing a form of critical clinical impotence. Again and again the movies returned to the spectacle of men who try and fail or don't try but fail anyway, who cannot relate to women as anything but objects of fear, mystery, or desire, and who are left – with startling consistency – at their story's end with nowhere to go but on to the next and possibly fatal fuck-up.

This much was true, but what remained to be questioned was whether all this fabricated dramatic failure amounted to a form of cultural failure – whether it was fair to blame the films and filmmakers for expressing something the culture was uneasy admitting about itself. At bottom, a lot of the post-*Survival* critical commentary on the national cinema was as idealistic and prescriptive as Pete and Joey were when they set out for a Toronto that they assumed would be theirs for the taking. And whose fault was that? The boys for their absurdly childish and optimistic naivety? Or the social and economic conditions that let such dreams flourish even in the complete absence of any real-life reinforcement?

This was the kind of thinking that began to emerge in the mid- to late 1970s, when *Road* and the movies that followed underwent a process of reconsideration based less on the cinema we thought we needed than on the cinema we had and what it told us, whether or not we wanted to hear it. By now perhaps, the years of unfulfilled breakthrough had generated a sense of realism more befitting the English Canadian cinema as both a cultural and commercial entity, and the time had come to reconsider the films in a more objective manner. And what was seen was something, well, distinctive.

Responding to the idea that Pete and Joey are somehow congenitally fated to failure, and thinking about that final act of Loblaws parking-lot desperation, critic Martin Knelman wrote, in *This Is Where We Came In* (1977): 'In fact the picture is practically a case-study of how people get to be criminals. Uprooted because of the country's failure to make one region as prosperous as another, they find themselves stripped of the social customs and institutions that have always given them their bearings. In the big city, the dream that lured them away from home – the prospect of material heaven suggested by slick magazines and TV commercials – proves to be cruelly beyond their reach. They can't blend into the background; out of their element, they're forced to exist as freaks in a ghetto culture for displaced Maritimers.'

For Knelman, the suggestion that Pete and Joey's travails were somehow self-generated, or produced by some kind of essential failure of character, was not only absurd but untrue. Looking back on Shebib's movie, he saw a film that was taking obvious pains to situate its characters in a very specific and systematic apparatus of socio-economic deprivation: 'Several critics have remarked that Canadian movies seem to be consistently about victims and losers; and undeniably, there is a measure of defeat in these tales about the ways people faced with cultural deprivation try to compensate, and the prices they pay when their ways out fail. Yet there is also often a kind of noble stubbornness – sometimes funny and sometimes touching – about plain people who, faced with a world that requires something more complicated than plainness for survival, still refuse to surrender their dreams.'[1]

A year earlier, Peter Harcourt had observed something similar in the work and characters of Don Shebib. Not quite 'noble stubbornness' perhaps, but a form of deeply seated questioning of their circumstances.

(Moreover, Harcourt insisted, 'Shebib's films are less about losers than they are about loners – like a good many Canadian films. And indeed, Canada is a country in which there is very little sense of people working together collectively – especially in Toronto where everybody seems to be working against everybody else.')[2] Most of the time, as Harcourt pointed out, this was only apparent in the silences that had come to abound and echo in Shebib's work: those moments, like the scene in *Goin' Down the Road* where Pete puts on the Satie record he bought at A&A's the night he saw the unattainable beauty haunting the classical department. Everyone just sits and stares, their unspoken thoughts – and our projected ideas of what they might be – forming the manifest dramatic content of the scene.

For Harcourt, such scenes were reflective of an artist, a sensibility, and perhaps even a culture that yearned to be and to have what it could not. According to Harcourt, it wasn't chronic failure that defined the boys as Canadians, it was their ultimately tragic conviction that there was always something else to be had. If only they knew how and if only they knew what. Yes, this is a state of restlessness, dissatisfaction, disappointment, and ultimate despair. But it comes from somewhere deep, deeper than just being too stupid to know better.

'At their centre,' Harcourt wrote of Shebib's films, 'there is always the sense of something not there – some kind of challenge, some kind of cohesiveness, something never directly specified that might make life meaningful. This longing is scarcely present in the words his characters exchange: it is more in the way they look at one another or in the way they simply stare off into empty space – especially the men. What are the qualities in life that hold people together, that might lead us collectively to a sense of identity or a feeling of purposefulness, a feeling of success? This is the question that, cumulatively, Shebib's films seem to ask.'[3]

For Harcourt the subject of Shebib's films wasn't Pete and Joey's failure to fulfil their dreams, it was the absence of some kind of communal connection or purpose that at once generated those dreams and thwarted them. In this sense, the Toronto depicted in the film is, as a symbol of Canadian experience, the symbol of the urban unravelling of any sense of a larger 'Canadian community.' It's not only where dreams come to die, but where the idea of a confederated Canadian experience is discarded, blown away, and kicked up and down the street like litter on Yonge.

True, it might not have been a pretty picture. But there was something honest about it and maybe even naked and profoundly true. 'As I have argued elsewhere,' Harcourt continued, 'perhaps in such a culture, it is wrong for us to expect from our cinema the normative values of psychological realism and narrative tidiness – characteristics possibly more germane to cultures that are surer of themselves, where individual roles are more securely defined. If at the present moment conditions of production and exhibition discourage the work of Don Shebib, it doesn't necessarily follow that it is *his* work that has to change.'

'The films of Don Shebib add up to a statement about life that seems appropriate to us as Canadians. His characters, especially his men, convey a vision of some better kind of life that might be possible elsewhere but *should* be possible here. Whether this is seen in class or cultural terms, this insight is real for us, for many of us, living here in Canada.'[4]

Increasingly, the acceptance of *Goin' Down the Road* as something incontrovertibly and essentially 'Canadian' appeared to be contingent on whether one accepted 'Canada' as it was. If one wished it was something else, if one wished one were somewhere else, one became the nationalist version of Harcourt's Pete and Joey: dreamers doomed forever to wake up right back here, instead of that vague and better elsewhere they only barely imagine.

For Christine Ramsay, who wrote extensively and incisively about *Goin' Down the Road* and its bumpy ride as a Canadian classic in the *Ca-*

nadian Journal of Film Studies in 1993, it was imperative that the movie be accepted for what it was: a nakedly honest and piercingly clear reflection of not only what Canada might have been at the time, but how preoccupied it was with becoming something else. For her, the ideas of nationhood and masculinity stem from the same desire to impose a structure and a centre upon something which in real life has neither. This is what myth, narrative, and popular culture do – they create ideal forms where none exist, and they project an imagined unity upon a fractured psychic, social, and cultural landscape. But the process of imagining these cohesive myths involves a form of necessary exclusion: on the one hand because some things do not – and can never – fit comfortably within the model, and on the other because the model itself needs difference in order to feel its own form, its own margins. In this context, Pete and Joey are the indigestibly marginalized. As Maritimers who don't fit, and as men who can't realize the hetero-male dream of conquest, confidence, and sexual potency.

For Ramsay, *Road* was fascinating, if not essential, precisely because it imagined a Canadian experience defined by longing, imagining, and disappointment. Indeed, it was about the limits and workings of Canada as a projected ideal, and the story was told from the outside: the outer frontier of what was permissibly Canadian. In this sense, the very process of criticizing the film for depicting 'losers' and 'failure' was a symptom of intellectual Pete and Joey-ism: like the boys, those who called for a different Canadian cinema – one with more confident men, more winning events, and happier endings – were themselves dreamers, wishing for something beyond what they had.

'I suspect,' Ramsay wrote, *'Goin' Down the Road* enjoys the status it does because of the uncanny precision with which it captures and demonstrates how English Canada constructs nation, sees culture, and experiences its sense of social self around an acute awareness of diversity, the de-centred centre, the periphery, the margins.'[5]

The film was a reflection after all, but the mirror it held up was, at least at a certain moment in Canadian cultural nationalist history, not reflecting an image many wished to see. Ramsay sees the processes of projecting 'nation' and 'masculinity' as inextricably co-dependent and intertwined, and Shebib's movie captured that co-dependency – and its pathology – with 'uncanny precision.' Indeed, *Road* was not only a Canadian classic, but classically Canadian, provided one understood Canada less as a geographical place than a rugged kind of dreamscape. If there was heroism apparent, and if one still needed to call it that, then maybe Pete, Joey, and Shebib *were* heroic. After all, they were demonstrating the balls to show something about living in their country that their country didn't want to look at.

'I put *Goin' Down the Road* forward as a valuable Canadian cinematic text because it lets the problems with "the nation" and masculinity show. Arguing against Atwood, Hofsess, and Fothergill, I think that this kind of minority discourse should not merely be judged a bad thing that promotes "negativity" in our self-perception; rather, it should be celebrated and studied for what it offers as a "performative space" for the representation of our social self – for what it offers as a lived text that makes intelligible to us, as English Canadians, from the position of the margins, the unique way we have historically faced the problems of social and personal identity through the Western concepts of "the nation" and omnipotent masculinity.'[6]

By the time Ramsay wrote this, there were fewer voices calling for a more thematically affirmative national cinema. This might partly be attributed to the passing of a particular moment in Canadian cultural nationalist thought – when telling artists to buck up and lighten up a little no longer seemed productive or reasonable – and it may also reflect a shift in intellectual paradigms. As Ramsay's piece suggests, by the early 1990s, culture itself was being seen less as a willed projection of desired values than as a product of the social, economic, and political forces which compel its existence. Once again, if Pete and Joey were losers, they were no longer born that way. They were made.

Besides, as the theoretical and scholarly scope of English Canadian cinematic criticism widened and, as years went by, the conditions of production changed and the sheer number of Canadian movies piled up, it seemed increasingly futile to make the argument that the movies would somehow be improved – or become more popular – if they grew a pair, kicked some ass, lived happily ever after, or just got over it.

Because they couldn't. On just about every one of these levels, they couldn't. In less than a decade after the release of *Goin' Down the Road*, the funding structures for Canadian film had been shifted almost entirely towards the production of domestically made Hollywood knock-offs, and this period – variously known as the Capital Cost Allowance or tax shelter eras – remains noteworthy primarily for the epic scale of the commercial failure of the movies it produced. We might have produced dozens of movies in which heroes acted heroically, got the girl, and left the losing to the losing side – and who were often played by stale-dated American stars like Lee Majors, Robert Mitchum, James Coburn, Elliott Gould, or Keir Dullea – but the movies themselves, for the most part, were utterly forgettable and flagrantly inauthentic. Moreover, those that did succeed – and spectacularly so – like Ivan Reitman's *Meatballs* and Bob Clark's *Porky's* – were hardly successes because they provided stirring populist paradigms of actualized, or comically inadequate, masculine behaviour. If anything, they connected because they transformed the tradition of arrested heterosexual male sexual development into the stuff of sophomoric comedy. (More on this later, when we get to the sublime 1982 *SCTV* parody, produced the same year that *Porky's* was released, of *Road*.)

With the collapse of the CCA model, a new generation of English Canadian auteurs emerged and, although notably distinct in terms of practice and style, their work was remarkably consistent in its depiction of psychic, spiritual, and cultural alienation. David Cronenberg, Atom Egoyan, Bruce McDonald, Patricia Rozema, John Paizs, Guy Maddin: the films of all these filmmakers, each of whom would enjoy significant degrees of international prominence and critical favour, were movies that traded in spectacles of concerted dysfunction. Populated by mutants, somnambulists, nerds, misfits, and voyeurs, the films were so emphatic in their denial of classically heroic figures and narratives that they amounted to a compelling argument that there was something in the 'Canadian' creative imagination that conspicuously resisted the cathartic mechanisms of Hollywood-style mass entertainment.

Cronenberg, who had been the subject of an aggressively dismissive column by Robert Fulford (who suggested the director, then making highly idiosyncratic and commercially successful made-in-Canada horror movies, ought not to qualify for public funds), was evolving into a formidably sui generis filmmaker, whose seminally influential 1982 movie *Videodrome* depicted Toronto as a kind of insatiable satellite dish pulling down malevolent – as in literally assaulting mind and body – broadcasting signals from a conspiratorial international media conglomerate. Egoyan, equally fixated on media-generated, externally imposed forms of alienation, cast the tape-and-erase properties of home videocassette (in *Next of Kin*, *Family Viewing*, and *Speaking Parts*) recording as a form of identity obliteration.

McDonald, going so far as to adopt Shebib's road-movie form in (the aptly titled) *Roadkill*, *Highway 61*, and *Hard Core Logo*, brought an absurdist and self-consciously ironic tone to the trip: his were road movies populated by singularly oblivious and direction-challenged travellers and, perhaps most significantly, reversed the urban-rural trajectory of *Road*. In these films, McDonald's protagonists – like those in *Rip-Off*, leave the city for the vast landscape, only to inevitably collide with their own delusions. From his ambivalently beloved Winnipeg, Maddin created a body of work that combined fetishistic retro-baroque, silent-era stylings – as far from docu-dramatic realism as one can get – with stories of narcolepsy, amnesia, obsession, and dangerously compressed sexual repression.

And so on. This was the new Canadian cinema that emerged after the Capital Cost Allowance fiasco and in the vacuum of a commercially driven English Canadian movie industry whose engine never quite turned over. If it looked radically different from Shebib's Bolex-grainy blend of documentary and fiction, in existential matters it was strikingly consistent.

It was through this cinematic prism that Ramsay wrote 'Canadian Narrative Cinema from the Margins,' and it permitted an interpretation of Shebib's movie not as a failure of what ought to be but as an instance of what so obviously was. Just as Ramsay saw the movie's tracking of Pete and Joey's tragedy as a frank depiction of a systemically unequal social apparatus, and interpreted the film as an act of artistic resistance against the falsely affirmative codes of popular Hollywood cinema, so these newer films seemed to carry on that calculated spirit of dire refusal.

Besides, if one looked further back and more widely afield, it became apparent that it certainly wasn't Shebib who gave birth to the all-Canadian loser figure in film. He was born before Shebib came along and offered him a lift to Toronto, and he had already travelled at least as far east as Quebec. Indeed, one of the most arresting contradictions in the entire Anglo-Canadian loser debate was the fact that while many critics, filmmakers, and students of Canadian film had looked enviously to Québécois cinema as a model of a thriving, distinctive, and culturally competitive 'national' cinema, that cinema was also profoundly prone to the depiction of hardship, marginality, failure, and despair. If the 'radical inadequacy' of the hetero-male character in English Canadian movies was cause for a kind of prescriptive alarm, matters would certainly seem to be even more urgent in the films of Quebec. That it wasn't says something not only about the arguably colonized sensibilities of English Canadian critics writing about English Canadian movies, but also about the sheer legitimacy of Ramsay's argument that many Canadian filmmakers couldn't help but make movies that displayed a profound disinclination towards the triumphant individualist codes of the dominant American cinema. If culture was to be accepted as a reflection of the conditions in which people lived, Canadian culture – both French and English – reflected a society consistently attempting to work out its role as a marginalized entity in an increasingly globalized American media marketplace. *Goin' Down the Road* was enduringly contextualized as a primary text in the ongoing debate over what constitutes Canadian-ness, and this process – more prescriptive than descriptive – imposed readings on the film which probably distorted more than they illuminated. It could be that Pete and Joey were losers simply because they *couldn't* be heroes. Their road didn't lead to Hollywood.

If anything, we came by losing honestly. It was our way of asserting an independent identity. It was who we were.

Pete, Joey, Garth, Gord, and Jesus Too

Apart from the New Yorker Theatre opening in Toronto in July 1969, the most significant date in the cultural history of *Goin' Down the Road* was 5 November 1982. That's the night when *SCTV Television*, a Canadian-born TV parody program then in its fourth season – and being broadcast by a US network for the first time – aired *Garth and Gord and Fiona and Alice*, a take-off of *Goin' Down the Road* so sublimely effective, subtly observed, and howlingly funny it marked a turning point in the original film's legacy. Once aired, it became almost impossible to think of Shebib's movie without referencing *GGFA*.

If anything, the mere existence of the parody – in the context of a program premised on the idea that a disruptive janitorial strike at the fictional SCTV Network prompted the station to air content from the cheapest available programming substitute – the CBC – was proof that Shebib's movie had been absorbed sufficiently into the pop cultural consciousness to resonate in parodic form. This is an interesting presumption in itself, considering that the movie was by then twelve years old, barely available on videotape, and only sporadically visible on TV.

What elevated the parody from the status of merely interesting to borderline perverse was the fact that most of the audience wasn't even Canadian and had virtually no familiarity with the original movie the take-off was taking off. Add to that the context of the episode's overall repertoire of made-in-Canada, public broadcasting TV cheddar – *Monday Night Curling*, two of whose three hosts are named Gord, *Hinterland Who's Who*, *Headline Challenge*, etc. – and one begins to appreciate not only how endemically Canadian *SCTV* was, but how brazenly so. A mortifyingly deadpan *Front Page Challenge* parody on US network TV? Curling? A shot-for-shot send-up on *Hinterland Who's Who*? *Magnum P.E.I.*? A singularly uneventful NFB stop-motion chestnut by 'Norman McClaren' called *The Chair*? *Goin' Down the Road*? The cheek was jaw-dropping.

Even more impressive was the fact that the primary instigator of the episode (which became legendary as 'The Canadian Show') was *SCTV's* only non-Canadian, Joe Flaherty. A Pittsburgh-born Toronto transplant who was one of the original members of the Toronto Second City franchise, where he worked with his future sister-in-law – and *Road* parody co-star – Jayne Eastwood, Flaherty was obviously richly amused by what so many Canadians merely took for granted: the stultifyingly dull, high-fibre nature of so much of their domestic television diet, and the often hair-raisingly stark contrast between what Canadians produced for themselves and what got beamed at them from south of the border. It was one of those cracks in the national experience that couldn't help but create a certain bipolarity in the 'national identity,' and it was a defining condition of the entire *SCTV* parodic *gestalt*.

The paths leading to this re-ignition of *Road's* cultural engine are worth noting, for they track what would become a significantly influential convergence of Canadian pop cultural currents. Two years after making *Road*, Jayne Eastwood auditioned for a role in *Godspell*, a chipper, clown-faced musical interpretation of the Gospel According to St Matthew. The show was a hit, running for nearly five hundred performances and variously including a cast of performers who would go on to become the nucleus of the coming decade's big bang of TV sketch comedy: future *SCTV* members Eugene Levy, Andrea Martin, Martin Short, and Dave Thomas were featured in *Godspell*, as was *Saturday Night Live's*

Gilda Radner. Paul Shaffer, future bandleader for David Letterman, was the show's musical conductor.

In spring 1973, Eastwood and Radner left the show to join the newly formed Toronto Second City troupe, which also included Flaherty, Dan Aykroyd, and future SCTV executive producer Andrew Alexander. The following year, John Candy, Catherine O'Hara, and Eugene Levy joined the Toronto troupe, followed by Andrea Martin and Dave Thomas in 1975, and finally Martin Short in 1977. That puts almost the entire cast of SCTV on the Toronto Second City stage, and in *Godspell* before that, with Jayne Eastwood.

Shebib's film was definitely an object of veneration for at least some of these up-and-coming Canadian sketch-comedy stars, a movie which conceivably contributed not only to a sense of local cultural continuity but to 'Canadian' culture itself. You'll recall Levy's memory of Eastwood's status among the *Godspell* hopefuls, which is indicative of just how visible the film was for that emerging generation of performers – just how must-see it once was. (Incidentally, the star of Shebib's second feature, *Rip-Off*, was Don Scardino, the second actor to play *Godspell*'s boy-clown Jesus.)

Thus, nine years after the formation of the Toronto Second City troupe, it was not surprising that the SCTV company would still be thinking about *Road* when they got thinking about iconically über-Canuck experiences to parody, or that Flaherty – whose brother Eastwood had by then married – would recruit the original Bets to reprise her role – and revive her beehive – in *Garth and Gord and Fiona and Alice*.

The parody is a work of some wonder. Condensing but capturing the essential narrative of *Road*, *GGFA* begins with Garth (John Candy), an out-of-work Maritime lawyer, pulling up in his hand-painted convertible jalopy at the doors of the 'Maritime General Hospital,' which looks more than suspiciously (and certainly deliberately) like the loading dock of a warehouse. There he almost instantly convinces Gord (Flaherty, sporting a Bradley-high pompadour) to come to Toronto where there's tons of 'doctorin' jobs and lawyerin' jobs.'[1]

On the way they sing, smoke, drink beer, and eat raw fish with idiot glee, pulling over somewhere between the Atlantic and the Don Valley to pick up Fiona Cornuyer (Andrea Martin), a French-Canadian nuclear physicist who's heard there's lots of jobs for them there too. The lads ask her to hop in, rounding out the ticket for their Oz-bound failure tour.

Arriving in the Emerald City, Garth gets on a payphone to let his friend Larry know they're in town looking for work and they've picked up an exotic animal on the way. 'She's a nuclear physicist! And she's French!' screeches Candy, echoing Pete's first eyeballing of the sumptuous Nicole.

'French, Larry! *French!* Do you hear me?'

Like bugs drawn to illuminated zappers, they converge on Yonge Street for the first of several displays of almost prostrate yokel delight at the strip's cheaply illuminated allure. 'Yonge Street!' they howl at the very idea. *'Yonge Street!'*

On the strip they meet Alice (Eastwood), who has just moved into the dingy little pad they've rented when Gord announces – after disappearing with her into an adjacent room for maybe six seconds – that's she's pregnant. 'Oh Gord,' whines Eastwood in an amped-up Bets voice that mangles words like 'house' and 'about' until they rhyme with 'moose' and 'a hoot.' 'What are we gunna *do?*'

A pause, distinctly Leiterman-esque in its close-up silence, then Gord looks at Garth. 'Yonge Street!' he cries. *'Yonge Street!'*

After Fiona eagerly splits for a job at the Hazelton Bowling Lanes, Garth, Alice, and Gord sit around staring abjectly at the walls, and the parody pays perhaps its most precise but subtly arcane tribute to the original. It's a take-off of the moment when Pete plays the Satie record he bought the night he saw the unattainable angel in A&A's, and he and

Bets and Joey simply sit in silence and listen, the room filling with music and unspoken sadness. Here it is again, reconfigured as a moment of startlingly surgical parody.

Unlike Pete and Joey, however, Garth and Gord don't stay sad for long. They're too dumbly happy to entertain a bum-out (or '*oot*,' actually) for any longer than it takes to decide to return to Yonge Street (!) one final time before hitting the road once again and heading westward. As Gordon Lightfoot's 'Alberta Bound' foot-taps them out, *Garth and Gord and Fiona and Alice* concludes, the credits – white on blue, just like the original – run, proudly reminding us that what we've just seen was 'Filmed entirely in Canada, by Canadians, for Canadians. Distributed by American International Pictures.'

At the first opportunity she could, Eastwood arranged to have the parody shown to Shebib, whom she remembers 'laughing so hard I thought he was going to die.'[2] William Fruet heard about it and made a point of catching it in reruns, and his first response was 'How dare they? This is *ours* and they're making fun of it,' but he subsequently surrendered and learned to love what SCTV had done.[3] In California, McGrath heard about the parody for years before he actually saw it, when he was bowled over. 'It was brilliant,' he told me in 2011. 'Absolutely brilliant.'[4]

Moreover, it confirmed something perhaps more convincingly than the movie itself: a legacy, legitimacy, and currency, a kind of perverse but potent proof that Pete, when he had lamented to Joey in a Yonge Street tavern that 'it's all for nuttin',' had managed to make at least one dream stick. He'd wanted to leave something behind that said 'Peter McGraw was there.' Among other things, the SCTV parody – which still appears in syndicated reruns nearly thirty years on – proved the guy had left his mark.

Further

In the first flush of release, just about everyone involved in making *Goin' Down the Road* entertained dreams of fame and glory, but they forgot where they were: Toronto in 1970, the very one which had figured so prominently, and indifferently, in the movie itself.

The movie played for a few months at the New Yorker, enjoyed a limited release across the country and in the United States, played on CBC television (which is where I remember seeing it and wondering, at the Hollywood-prone age of thirteen, what all the fuss was about), then did what most movies did in those days when their theatrical run sputtered. It disappeared.

Whatever dreams of national stardom Doug McGrath might have entertained rather quickly evaporated because he still couldn't get gigs at places like the CBC because he didn't speak, as he put it to me, 'Shek-spiddian.'[1] He worked in Canada for the next few years in supporting parts – appearing in Fruet's *Wedding in White* and Bob Clark's *Black Christmas* – before going to the United States, finding frequent work on the dusty margins of Clint Eastwood westerns.

Jayne Eastwood went from *Road* to *Godspell* to *Second City*, thence to TV, where she appeared in literally thousands of hours of Canadian variety shows, commercials, and episodic dramas, more than one episode of which was directed by Don Shebib.

Having made the shift from documentary to dramatic cinematography, Richard Leiterman made it his primary professional domain, shooting some of English Canada's most visually impressive features over the next couple of decades: *Rip-Off* and *Between Friends* for Shebib, *Who Has Seen the Wind* and *Silence of the North* for Allan King, *My American Cousin*, *Ticket to Heaven*, and *Surfacing*. But he too found his steadiest work in TV, eventually turning to teaching until his untimely death in 2005.

Bill Fruet hired Leiterman to shoot the movie of his play *Wedding in White* in 1972, and also hired Bradley and McGrath to appear as the two coward-bully-clownish drunkards who leave such an ugly mess behind when they blow through the prairie town in which the movie is set. Although it was nearly as positively received as *Road* itself was, and launched the screenwriter's long dreamed-of career as a director, he too wound up TV-bound after making a couple of considerably more commercial and comparatively less remarkable features. He remained in TV until his recent semi-retirement.

As is captured in Shebib's 1972 documentary portrait *Born Hustler*, Paul Bradley emerged from *Goin' Down the Road* with a rather full tank of optimism-enriched gas. In the movie, he's seen driving around Toronto in a rented limo, talking up his career and brilliant future to just about anybody who'll listen, which never amounts to an audience much larger than the director, cinematographer, and editor, Don Shebib.

Plagued with a lifelong drinking problem, Bradley, the actor whom just about everyone involved in *Road* thought was most surely destined for great things, found it increasingly hard to find work in Toronto or anywhere. Eastwood remembered him showing up at her home and catastrophically mixing alcohol and lighter fluid. McGrath remembered Bradley visiting periodically and always without prior announcement, once showing up in Calgary where his former co-star was performing, and once – at three a.m. – honking his horn in front of McGrath's Los Angeles house. Shebib hired Bradley a couple of times for TV episodes, but the booze was becoming harder and harder to forgive. After auditioning unsuccessfully for *Saturday Night Live* in 1975, Bradley pretty much disappeared. Occasionally his *Road* fellow travellers would hear from him, or would hear that he'd been spotted here, there, or elsewhere in Canada, but that was about it. The first news they heard in many years about Paul Bradley was in 2003. He had died in Vancouver.

Don Shebib was still making movies at the time of this writing. He was seventy-three years old when I sat down for a lengthy interview in his home in 2011, and he was putting the finishing touches on a sequel of sorts to *Goin' Down the Road* called *Down the Road Again*.

He was generous, courteous, and thoughtful in the interview process, but in no way had mellowed. His legendary cantankerousness towards his industry, his country, and his critics was right out front. He can't help himself, even if it has cost him dearly in professional terms.

'Canadian producers have shunned me like the fucking plague,' he said, as if it were mysterious. He went on: 'If a producer whom I think makes bad films doesn't like my script, well why would he like it? He wouldn't know a good script if he fucked it. So how many really wonderful Canadian scripts have been rejected by producers because they didn't see how good it was? And it happens all the time. And so if somebody thinks it's bad that's good because what they think is good is not.'[2]

It seemed a good time to broach the subject of fleeting Canadian fame, and he told me a story. 'This is funny,' he said. 'I'm a very serious, obsessive person. If it isn't golf it's football or it's stamp collecting. And I was a serious model airplane maker. One time I was in a model shop, this was twenty years ago when I did a lot of serious modelling, this guy comes in and he says "Oh, you're Don Shebib, eh? I'm really pleased to meet you. I loved your last work. That was fabulous. That Galloping Ghost was incredible!"'

Shebib looked at the guy. 'Galloping Ghost?'

'I had no idea what he was talking about. Then I realized I built a

P-51 Mustang, and on the side was painted "Galloping Ghost." He didn't know anything about my filmmaking. But he knew the Galloping Ghost. I still have it upstairs. A P-51 Mustang with a chequered front. He didn't know anything about my filmmaking, he didn't know anything about me as a filmmaker, but he knew me as a model maker.'[3]

The sequel idea had been raised before. It was something Shebib had been resisting until he was talked into it by Cayle Chernin, the Eli Rill alumna who'd appeared as Bets's friend Selena in the original movie.

Chernin had pitched the sequel idea primarily as a tribute to Bradley, whose posthumous spirit could infuse the movie as a kind of ignition-turning motivation for Pete to get back behind the wheel of that Canadian Shield–solid junker of an Impala. Shebib was wooed by Chernin, got to work on the script, and shot the movie in 2010–11, more than forty years after he'd first hit the city streets with his skeleton crew, dedicated cast, and a few thousand dollars back in 1969.

Much has changed since then, and much has not. Don Shebib, for instance. When asked what he expected to happen with the sequel, he said he had no idea if anyone would want to see the movie, or if anyone ever would. And that's more or less exactly what he said way back then.

Epilogue: Down the Road Again

Goin' Down the Road is a movie of unfinished business and unresolved ambitions. It's all about what doesn't happen. In the end, Pete and Joey leave Toronto with their dreams in pieces. They have been caught breaking the law, clobbered an interfering grocery clerk with a tire iron, and leave the pregnant Bets behind. We can only imagine how much pain and guilt they carry on the road west, but it seems a lot.

Down the Road Again, the sequel to his first movie that Don Shebib made in 2011, is haunted by that pain and strives to make it better. Thirty-some years on Pete (Doug McGrath again), now working as a postal worker in suburban Vancouver, evidently carries more than letters in his bag. It's obvious in the slump in his shoulders, the effort in his step, and the sag of his old-dog face: Pete has lived alone with his memories and regrets for a lifetime now, but the heaviest piece of mail he'll ever handle comes with the news that Joey has died.

The letter comes with instructions: from the grave, Joey wants Pete to disinter the old Impala (miraculously even for Vancouver, it's been kept intact under a garage tarp for all these years), drive it to Toronto to deliver another letter from Joey to Bets (Eastwood again), and proceed all the way to Cape Breton to spread Joey's ashes in the Atlantic. Muttering Popeye-like to himself (just as Joey's letter talks to him on the soundtrack), Pete takes destiny by the throttle and hits the gas.

Pete (Doug McGrath) hits the road again in Donald Shebib's *Down the Road Again*. Photo credit: Caitlin Cronenberg. Courtesy of Union Pictures.

By the time Joey's ashes are distributed windward, Pete has made peace with the past. He and Bets have resolved their decades of simmering resentment, he and Joey's grown-up daughter Betty-Jo (Kathleen Robertson) have established a surrogate father–daughter relationship, and Pete has learned something he never knew: Joey had a secret that prevented him from speaking up when Pete insisted they dump Betty and flee the city. So the burden of guilt Pete's carried all these years is, if not lifted, at least partly blown away with his old buddy's ashes.

This overriding drive for resolution, the cross-country, multi-generational pursuit of reassurance and reconciliation, is the most curious thing about *Down the Road Again*. The narrative engine is powered by the desire to leave characters in that state of assisted peace called closure, to bring to a destination a journey that, for over four decades now, was so haunting precisely because it never arrived anywhere. Those guys stayed with you because they had nowhere else to go.

There was also something painfully truthful about that lack of destination, or at least painfully true to the circumstances depicted. These were men who had gone to Toronto on a delusion, and the hard poignancy of the movie's message was that the delusion died hard. Pete and Joey were part of an westward migration of the economically and culturally displaced, and *Goin' Down the Road* was the sad ballad of what a country can do to its people when it takes away their livelihood, their culture, and their hopes and then leaves them in the ditch.

Road's lack of emotional resolution wasn't a shortcoming. It was essential to what the movie was saying about Canada in 1969. This was a country that had learned not to care about people like Pete and Joey. When they hightailed it all the way west they needed no reason other than desperation, so it might come as a surprise to some viewers of the sequel to see a reason provided. Perhaps even more curious is that the reason isn't social or economic but personal, as if the whole ordeal of the first movie was just a bad dream that a letter from a dead man can make go away after all these years.

The untidy conclusion of *Goin' Down the Road* was perfect, in other words, and perfectly true to the reality Shebib and his cast and crew simulated so convincingly. Moreover, it was an untidiness that wasn't restricted to story and character: it was in the washed-out graininess of the blown-up 16-mm footage, the on-the-fly vérité camerawork of Richard Leiterman, the unarranged faces of real people caught in the lens, and the unaffected naturalism of the performances. *Everything* was untidy, and that's what made the movie so memorable and affecting: like spray from a curb-side mud puddle, it stained you with a cold, sloppy splash of reality.

Down the Road Again is tidiness itself: carefully composed and comfortably lit, controlled in tone, and precisely measured in effect. You can see Shebib's decades of experience in it and, were it not for its notably unfashionable embrace of high sentiment, the movie fits snugly within the universe of family-friendly TV entertainment that is its most likely destination. It does not leap out and it does not linger in memory. It is unlikely, in other words, to convince many of us that things worked out all right for Pete and Joey just because we might have wished they did. But we can all dream, can't we?

Production Credits

Director

Donald Shebib

Writer

William Fruet

Cast

Pete	Doug McGrath
Joey	Paul Bradley
Betty	Jayne Eastwood
Selena	Cayle Chernin
Nicole	Nicole Morin
Frenchy	Pierre La Roche

Producer

Donald Shebib

Original Music Score

Bruce Cockburn

Cinematographer

Richard Leiterman

Sound

James McCarthy

Editor

Donald Shebib

Running Time

90 minutes

Aspect Ratio

133:1

Further Viewing

Between Friends. Donald Shebib. Clearwater Films, 1973.

Born Hustler. Donald Shebib. Canadian Broadcasting Corporation, 1972.

Down the Road Again. Donald Shebib. Union Pictures, 2011.

Easy Rider. Dennis Hopper. Columbia Pictures, 1969.

Good Times Bad Times. Donald Shebib. Canadian Broadcasting Corporation, 1969.

The Grapes of Wrath. John Ford. Twentieth-Century Fox, 1939.

Hard Core Logo. Bruce McDonald. Shadow Shows, 1996.

Midnight Cowboy. John Schlesinger. United Artists, 1969.

You Only Live Once. Fritz Lang. Walter Wanger Productions, 1937.

Notes

Prologue: A Heavy Rainbow

1 Interview with Don Shebib, 2011.
2 The scholarly work on *Goin' Down the Road* has been extensive, but much of it is no longer in print. Apart from those works directly cited in the text of this book and pertinent to its aims, the following, which also address the film's status, meaning, and legacy, were consulted: Geoff Pevere et al., *Toronto on Film* (Toronto: Wilfrid Laurier University Press, 2009); Chris Gittings, *Canadian National Cinema* (New York: Routledge, 2002); Peter Dickinson, *Screening Gender, Framing Gender: Canadian Literature into Film* (Toronto: University of Toronto Press, 2007); George Melnyk, ed., *One Hundred Years of Canadian Cinema* (Toronto: University of Toronto Press, 2004); R. Bruce Elder, *Image and Identity* (Waterloo: Wilfrid Laurier University Press, 1989); Piers Handling, ed., *Self-Portrait: Essays on the Canadian and Quebec Cinemas* (Ottawa: Canadian Film Institute, 1980).

1. Surfing from Scarborough

1 Pierre Berton, *The Pierre Berton Show*, 1972. Episode included on 2002 *Goin' Down the Road* DVD release by Seville Pictures.
2 Interview with Don Shebib, 2011.
3 Ibid.
4 Ibid.
5 Don Shebib, *Pierre Berton Show*.

6 Ibid.
7 Shebib interview.
8 Shebib, *Pierre Berton Show*.
9 Shebib interview.
10 Ibid.
11 Ibid.
12 Ibid.
13 Ibid.
14 Ibid.
15 Peter Harcourt, 'Men of Vision: Some Comments on the Work of Don Shebib,' in *Canadian Film Reader*, ed. Seth Feldman and Joyce Nelson (Toronto: Peter Martin Associates, 1977), 210.
16 Ibid., 215.
17 Shebib interview.

2. Beginner's Licence

1 Piers Handling, *The Films of Don Shebib* (Ottawa: Canadian Film Institute, 1978), 99.
2 Interview with William Fruet, 2011.
3 Ibid.
4 Ibid.
5 John Hofsess, *Inner Views: Ten Canadian Film-Makers* (Toronto: McGraw-Hill Ryerson, 1975), 122.
6 Handling, *The Films of Don Shebib*, 99.
7 Interview with Jayne Eastwood, May 2011.
8 Fruet interview.
9 Interview with Douglas McGrath, May 2011.
10 Interview with Don Shebib, May 2011.
11 Fruet interview.
12 Ibid.
13 McGrath interview.
14 Ibid.
15 Ibid.
16 Eastwood interview.

17 Cayle Chernin, *Canadian Actor Online*, http://www.canadianactor.com/actors/pov/gdtr.html.

18 Ibid.

19 Eastwood interview.

20 Shebib interview.

21 Eastwood interview.

22 'Trial by Fire: A Journey with Richard Leiterman,' *Take One*, May 2002.

23 Norman Mailer, *The Armies of the Night: The Novel as History, History as a Novel* (New York: Plume, 1994), 136.

24 Alan Rosenthal, 'A Married Couple: An Interview with Allan King,' in *Canadian Film Reader*, ed. Seth Feldman and Joyce Nelson (Toronto: Peter Martin Associates, 1977), 184.

25 Ibid., 185.

26 Eastwood interview.

27 McGrath interview.

28 'Trial by Fire.'

29 Alison Reid and P.M. Evanchuck, *Richard Leiterman* (Ottawa: Canadian Film Institute, 1978), 59.

30 McGrath interview.

31 Fruet interview.

32 Handling, *The Films of Don Shebib*, 100.

33 Shebib interview.

34 McGrath interview.

3. The Road Rolls

1 On a website called 'The Cockburn Project' (http://cockburnproject.net/frames.html), there are passages that illuminate the contentious history of the music's origins and subsequent use. This comes from Jack Batten's January 1971 piece on Cockburn in *Maclean's*: 'A polite voice from out of the slight gloom of the War Memorial Auditorium in Guelph, Ontario, about tenth row centre, asks for a request. "Sing something from your movie," the voice calls, belonging, you can make it out, to a boy in his late teens. "From *Goin' Down The Road*, if you would." It's been the same request for the last six months, and Cockburn, alone on a stool in the spotlight, looks

patient. "I'm sorry," he says into his microphone in a soft and final voice. "I don't sing those songs. When I wrote them, I wrote them to express the point of view of the people in the movie. It isn't my point of view. It isn't me. So, you know, I can't sing them here."'

And this, from a Canoe Online chat with Cockburn dated January 2002. Cockburn is asked why the songs for the film were never included in an album: 'It was a subject of some controversy at the time. I'd never done a film score before and I was excited to do one because it was new but really I felt the songs I wrote for that were artificial. They were designed to be part of a film and so I elected not to record those songs whether on an album or on a soundtrack and that got me in all sorts of trouble with the director. There was a lot of bad feeling around it but that was my feeling at the time. I was probably more uptight about it than I needed to be but that's how I was in those days.'

2 Much of the movie's dialogue is included in the version of the shooting script published in 1992 as the first entry of *Best Canadian Screenplays*, a volume that also includes the scripts of *Mon Oncle Antoine*, *The Grey Fox*, *My American Cousin*, and *Jesus de Montréal*. But much of it isn't, which is what makes reading the shooting script both illuminating and fascinating. As Fruet freely admits, the script was frequently altered on the spot by Shebib according to the contingencies of the moment. Often the actors would improvise what the director felt were improvements on the written words – Peter's I-was-there tavern lesson in proto-Marxist alienation was one such case – and sometimes unforeseen events would transpire that were just too good to resist: the drunken singalong in Allan Gardens, for instance, or the freak October snowfall that lifted the flyer-delivering sequence into an unimagined realm of dreamy poignancy. Sometimes locations weren't available and had to be hastily replaced, and sometimes Shebib simply decided he'd rather try something different. In the end, even this process – that of using the script less as a roadmap than a compass – contributed to the film's scruffily convincing attitude of untucked vérité. Somehow, it feels less acted than lived.

Frequently, the changes and omissions seem to serve Shebib's sense of dramatic economy. When the boys first arrive in Toronto, for instance, Fruet's script has them pulled over by a cop alerted to potential trouble merely by the Nova Scotia licence plate. (Okay, maybe that and painted flames licking the Impala's side.) He runs a test on their plates and lets them go with this rather ominous warning: 'Okay, here are some of the hard facts of living in this city. We've got a lot of you boys coming here. No money, no jobs, no nothing. Most of you can't seem to stay out of trouble either. This is just a routine check with a little good advice thrown in – keep your nose clean … or else. Follow me?' One wonders if Shebib wisely felt the scene trumpeted a little too loudly and literally the coming fate of these guys and left it out. Because it certainly would have. Besides, when it comes to the ominous presence of the police in the movie, nothing speaks more eloquently than the silent passing of the real cop in the scene, much later, when Pete, Joey, and Bets are moving into the Cabbagetown flophouse. We certainly didn't need to be told what was going to happen to these guys before it happened in order to feel their tragedy, and it only would have dulled the film's edge of socio-economic disparity if the most prophetic words spoken on the subject came from a traffic cop. Follow me?

3 Amazingly, this sequence, one of the movie's most memorable, was apparently largely improvised. In the shooting script, the scene opens with the face of the advertising executive looking over Pete's application. Then he sits back and says, 'Whatever possessed you to come here for a job? I mean looking at this I can't see anything in your background to suggest even an interest in advertising.' The scene then ends.

4 Shebib shifted this scene, another of the movie's most indelible, from the shooting script's setting of the warehouse lunchroom to a tavern, which effectively lends Pete's lesson in dead-end economics an added atmosphere of futile desperation. No matter where he is, Pete can't stop thinking about how much better things ought to be.

5 Interestingly, the scene as written in the script has Nicole (still named Stella) dancing with a black man in 'The Trinidad Club' as Pete disconsolately looks on. When the man delivers her back to the table, she says to Pete, 'It was real swell of you to bring me. I always come here on a Friday night and I'd sure hate to miss it. These guys are just the greatest dancers. I mean they got such rhythm, you know?' Perhaps Shebib thought the added burden of racial resentment would only compromise our sympathy

for Pete, or maybe it just seemed like another unnecessarily heavy burden of impotence for Pete to bear. At any rate, in the scene as shot – Nicole's breasts at work in the foreground, Pete sipping on the sidelines – we don't have a clear view who she's dancing with and the point is still made. Pete isn't going to get laid.

6 In Fruet's shooting script, the just-married Bets and Joey have moved into 'a shabby old house on one of the rundown streets east of Yonge.' The shift to the new apartment building, with its view of the distant skyline, largely empty rooms, new, *TV Guide*-bought furniture and muzak on tap, perfectly embodies the precarious culture of no-money-down credit that will prove ultimately ruinous to the couple. It's their only real home, but only for as long as it takes for the bills to arrive. And the very fleeting nature of this brush with prosperity only intensifies the brutality of its loss.

7 This scene is much longer in Fruet's shooting script. Among other things deleted is Bets's presence when the boys first arrive. She's screaming hysterically as her furniture is taken to the sidewalk, and Joey pulls her into the car and drives off to her aunt's place. When he returns, Pete talks him into leaving Toronto for good. By already establishing that Bets has gone to her aunt's, Shebib makes her abandonment by Joey that much more sudden, brutal, and desperate. Not only does he not say goodbye, he is ultimately prevented from doing so by Pete – asserting his final act of dominance over Joey – while the poor woman is obviously sitting stricken somewhere waiting for a husband who will never show. As a denouement, it's considerably darker.

4. Is This the One?

1 Interview with Martin Knelman, 2011.
2 Interview with William Fruet, 2011.
3 Jim Beere, 'Goin' Down the Road a Great Canadian Movie,' *Toronto Star*, 3 July 1970.
4 Clyde Gilmour, 'Human Tale of Two Drifters in Toronto,' *Toronto Telegram*, 4 July 1970.
5 Kaspars Dzeguze, 'Go and See Goin' Down the Road: You'll Help Don She-

bib Pay for His New Sports Car and Encourage Him to Make More Movies,' *Maclean's*, September 1970.

6 Dane Lanken, 'Finally, the Great Canadian Movie,' *Montreal Gazette*, 8 August 1970.

7 Robert Fulford, 'Two Losers Lost in Cold Toronto,' *Saturday Night*, September 1970.

8 Interview with Jayne Eastwood, 2011.

9 Martin Knelman, *This Is Where We Came In: The Career and Character of Canadian Film* (Toronto: McClelland & Stewart, 1977), 11.

10 Piers Handling, *The Films of Don Shebib* (Ottawa: Canadian Film Institute), 3.

11 Interview with Robert Fothergill, 2011.

12 Judith Crist, *New York* magazine, 19 October 1970.

13 Pauline Kael, 'Men in Trouble,' *The New Yorker*, 31 October 1970.

14 Roger Greenspun, 'Goin' Down the Road Winds Its Way from Canada,' *New York Times*, 20 October 1970.

15 Roger Ebert, *Chicago Sun-Times*, 19 February 1971.

16 Dilys Powell, 'Gloomsday,' *Sunday Times*, 14 November 1970.

17 Piers Handling, *The Films of Don Shebib* (Ottawa: Canadian Film Institute, 1978), 2.

18 Interview with Piers Handling, 2011.

19 Ibid.

20 Interview with Robert Fothergill, 2011.

21 Handling interview.

22 Interview with Peter Harcourt, 2011.

23 John Hofsess, *Inner Views: Ten Canadian Film-Makers* (Toronto: McGraw-Hill Ryerson, 1975), 73–4.

5. Victims of the Rainbow

1 Margaret Atwood, *Survival: A Thematic Guide to Canadian Literature* (Toronto: McClelland & Stewart, 1972), 44.

2 Ibid., 43.

3 In *Canadian Film Reader* (Toronto: Peter Martin Associates, 1977).

4 Interview with Robert Fothergill, 2011.

5 Fothergill, 'Coward, Bully, or Clown,' 235–6.

6 Fothergill interview.

7 Fothergill, 'Coward, Bully, or Clown,' 237.

8 Interview with Peter Harcourt, 2011.

9 Ibid.

10 John Hofsess, *Inner Views: Ten Canadian Film-Makers* (Toronto: McGraw-Hill Ryerson, 1975), 36.

11 Ibid., 67–9.

12 Ibid., 77.

13 Ibid., 77–8.

14 Fothergill interview.

15 Ibid.

16 Interview with Don Shebib, 2011.

6. Re-surfacing

1 Martin Knelman, *This Is Where We Came In: The Career and Character of Canadian Film* (Toronto: McClelland & Stewart, 1977), 114.

2 Peter Harcourt, 'Men of Vision: Some Comments on the Work of Don Shebib,' in *Canadian Film Reader*, ed. Seth Feldman and Joyce Nelson (Toronto: Peter Martin Associates, 1977), 216.

3 Ibid., 215.

4 Ibid., 217.

5 Christine Ramsay, 'Canadian Narrative Cinema from the Margins: "The Nation" and Masculinity in Goin' Down the Road,' *Canadian Journal of Film Studies*, Autumn 1993, 34.

6 Ibid., 47.

7. Pete, Joey, Garth, Gord, and Jesus Too

1 'Garth and Gord and Fiona and Alice,' *SCTV volume 4* (DVD collection), Shout! Factory, 2006.

2 Interview with Jayne Eastwood, 2011.

3 Interview with William Fruet, 2011.

4 Interview with Douglas McGrath, 2011.

8. Further

1 Interview with Douglas McGrath, 2011.
2 Interview with Don Shebib, 2011.
3 Ibid.

Selected Bibliography

Atwood, Margaret. *Survival: A Thematic Guide to Canadian Literature.* Toronto: House of Anansi, 1972.

Bowie, Douglas, and Tom Shoebridge, eds. *Best Canadian Screenplays.* Kingston: Quarry Press, 1992.

Feldman, Seth, and Joyce Nelson, eds. *Canadian Film Reader.* Toronto: Peter Martin Associates, 1977.

Handling, Piers. *The Films of Don Shebib.* Ottawa: Canadian Film Institute, 1978.

Hofsess, John. *Inner Views: Ten Canadian Film-Makers.* Toronto: McGraw-Hill Ryerson, 1975.

Reid, Alison, and P.M. Evanchuk. *Richard Leiterman.* Ottawa: Canadian Film Institute, 1978.

Walz, Eugene P., ed. *Canada's Best Features: Critical Essays on 15 Canadian Films.* New York: Editions Rodopi, 2002.

CANADIAN CINEMA

Edited by Bart Beaty and Will Straw